AF262574

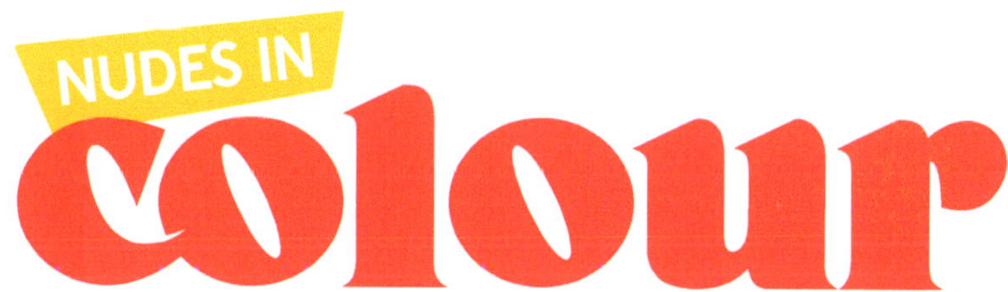

NUDES IN
colour

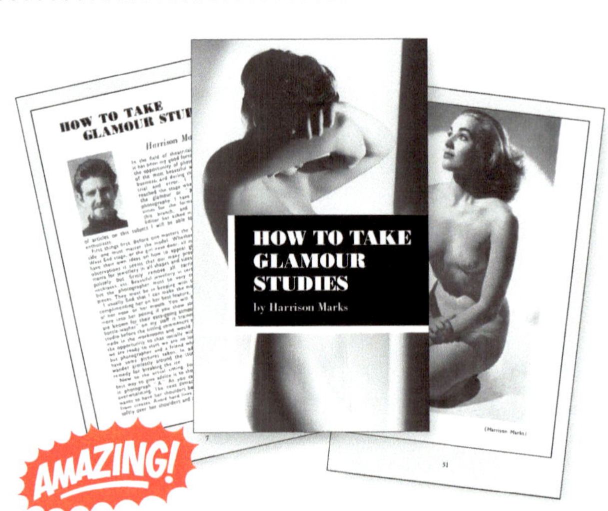

Published in 2024 by Wolfbait Books © 2024

www.wolfbait.co.uk

ISBN: 978-1-917298-06-3

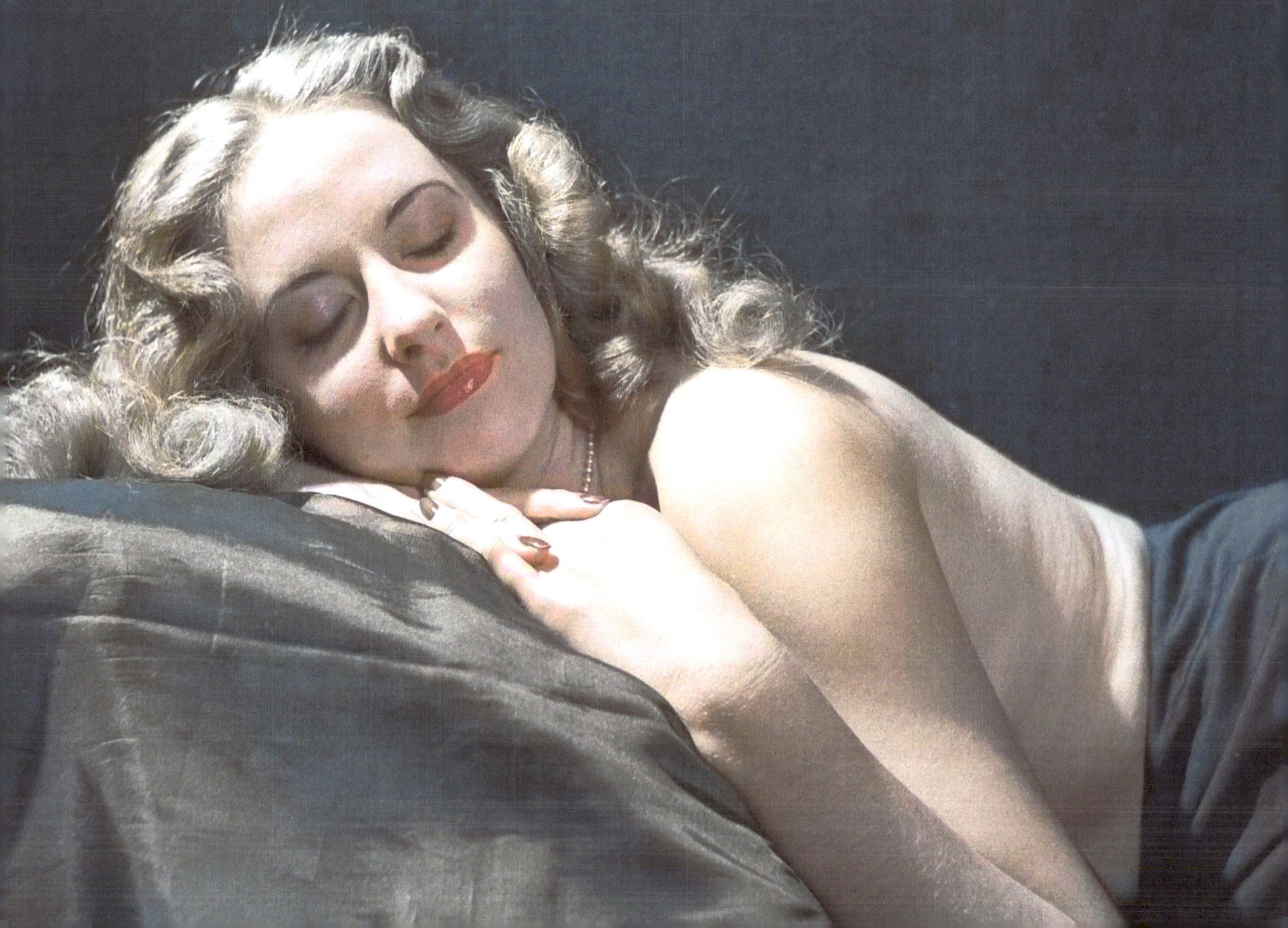

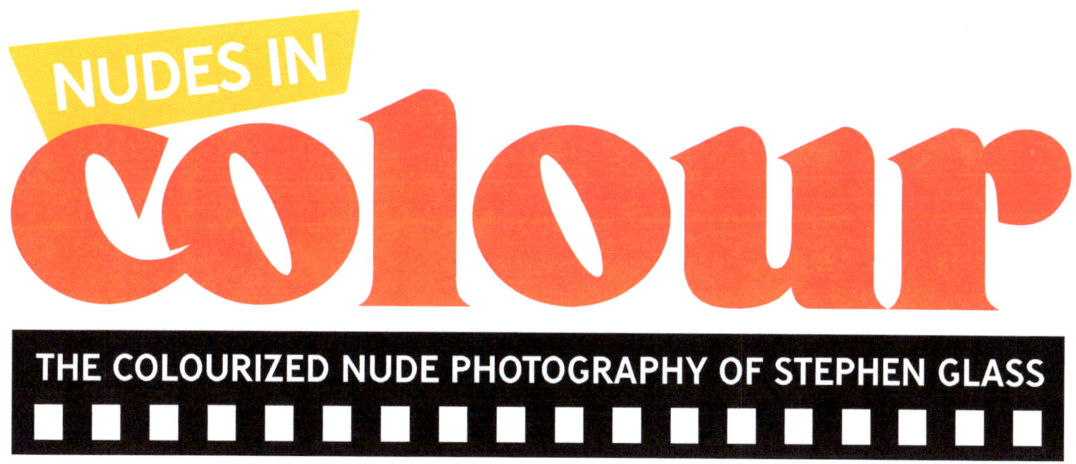

By Yahya El-Droubie

Photography by Stephen Glass

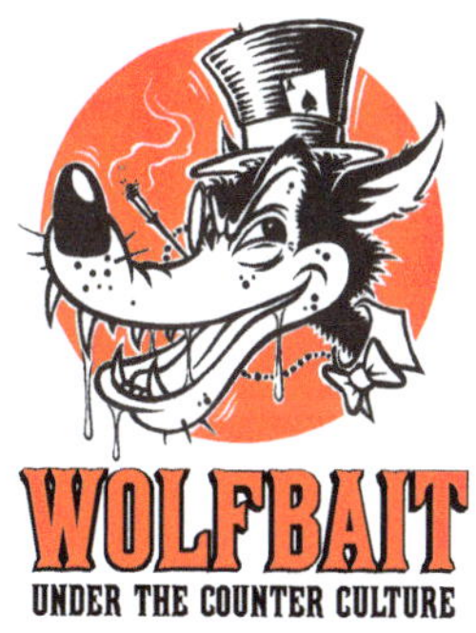

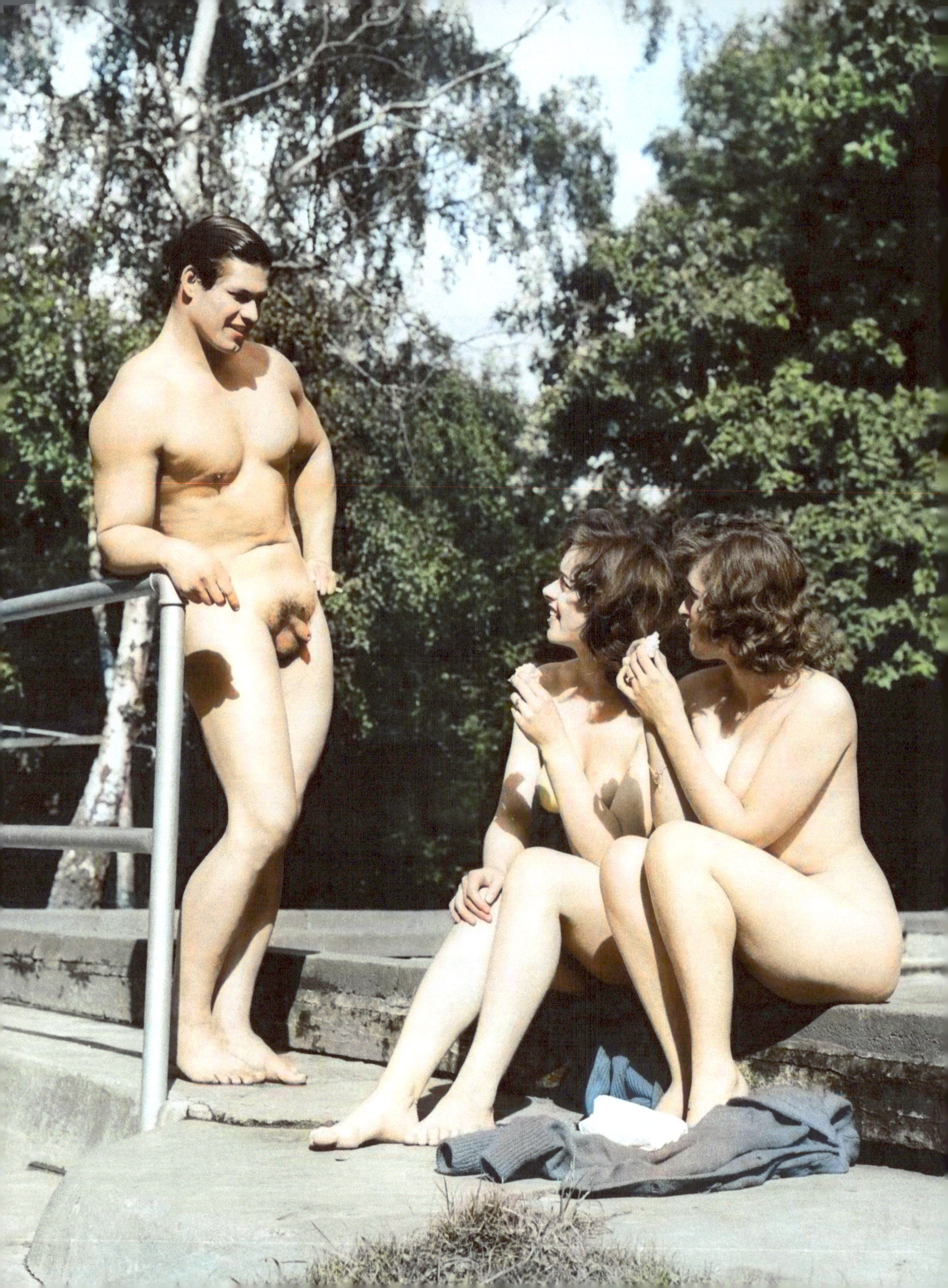

Introduction

THE HUNGARIAN PHOTOGRAPHER Stephen Glass is something of an enigma. During the 1950s his name was sufficiently well-known to be displayed prominently on magazine covers as a sales tool, but almost nothing was written about him or his work at that time. The opposite is true of his younger brother, Zoltán, who was also a photographer. Known to his friends as "Zolly", he was featured and interviewed in many magazines on both sides of the Atlantic.

History has recorded little about the Glass brothers' parents, Rezno and Olga, or the boys' early years, but what is known is that following three years of intensive study at commercial art schools in Budapest, Stephen earned a living as a designer, cartoonist, and painter. Zoltán was born in Budapest on April 26, 1903 and, following in his brother's footsteps, began his career as an artist and caricaturist. He struggled to make ends meet, however, and took various other jobs to supplement his income, among them docker, night watchman, photographic retoucher, and stage designer. He even dabbled in a spot of acting. In 1925, Zoltán moved to Berlin, Germany, where, like his brother, he was employed as a picture editor at an evening newspaper.

The Glass brothers prospered as members of a network of talented Hungarian émigrés. In 1930, Zoltán established Reclaphot, a photographic agency that specialised in advertising work, and Autophot, a company dedicated exclusively to automobile photography. The brothers would often work together. A keen motorsports enthusiast and amateur racer, Zoltán covered Germany's biggest races at the Nürburgring and Avus circuits. His most famous photographs are of the Mercedes-Benz Silver Arrows team, which dominated Grand Prix racing during the mid-1930s.

By 1936 doing business in Germany was becoming increasingly difficult for the brothers, who were Jewish, and they fled to London. Zoltán was given work by another Jewish refugee, Arthur Spingarn, the owner of Sackville Advertising;

When I cast off my clothes, I cast off my cares.
— Horace Walpole

however, as an enemy alien at the outbreak of World War II in 1938, he was not permitted to pursue his profession and faced the threat of internment. As a result, he voluntarily handed over his camera equipment to the British authorities.

After the war, Zoltán eked out a living taking publicity stills for clients in the film and theatre worlds. In 1948, after twelve years as an émigré, he became a naturalised British subject. It was around this time that Stephen began to concentrate on naturist photography.

Zoltán's career took a big step up when fellow Hungarian Arpad Elfer, creative director at Colman, Prentis and Varley, one of the most prestigious London advertising agencies, started giving him work. By the mid-1950s, he was one of the most successful fashion and advertising photographers in the capital, with a studio at 183 Kings Road, Chelsea, and another at 41 Paradise Walk, SW3.

One of Zoltán's clients was Odhams Press, which published *Lilliput*, a celebrated pocket-sized gentleman's magazine that featured an assortment of titillating articles and risqué humour, together with adventurous photographic essays by such well-known talents as Bill Brandt and Brassai. As Zoltán's reputation grew, he was dubbed "Picasso with a camera".

Meanwhile, Stephen made a name for himself taking pictures for continental magazines such as *Paris Hollywood, Femina,* and *Modelstudier.* However, he is best remembered for the work he did for *The Naturist* and *Health and Efficiency.*

In a rare interview he gave to *Health and Efficiency* magazine in 1951, Stephen confessed he was extremely interested in the fine arts and a keen sports enthusiast. Readers were also told that he played the cello and was an expert on physical training; at the time, he never missed his daily PT exercises and attended weightlifting and bodybuilding classes every week.

The well-known model Pamela Green (1929–2010) posed for both Glass brothers on several occasions: for Stephen at the infamous nudist camp Spielplatz in Hertfordshire, and at his tiny first-floor studio in Old Church Street in London's Chelsea, just off the King's Road. "In those days when Stephen photographed me, I still had dark hair," Pamela recalled. "He liked his props, especially the stuffed animals." Pamela's agent, Pearl Beresford, sent her along to Zoltán Glass,

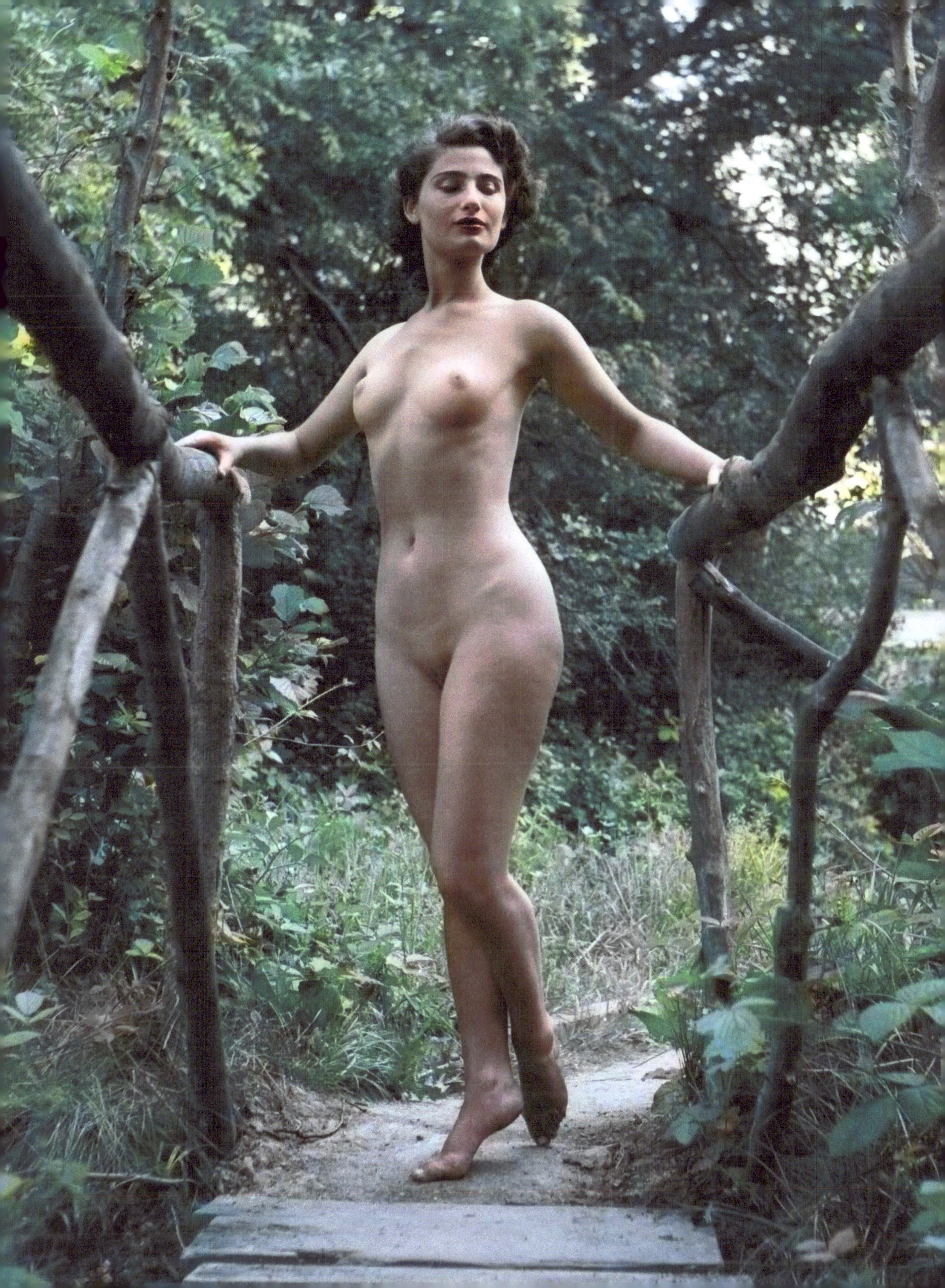

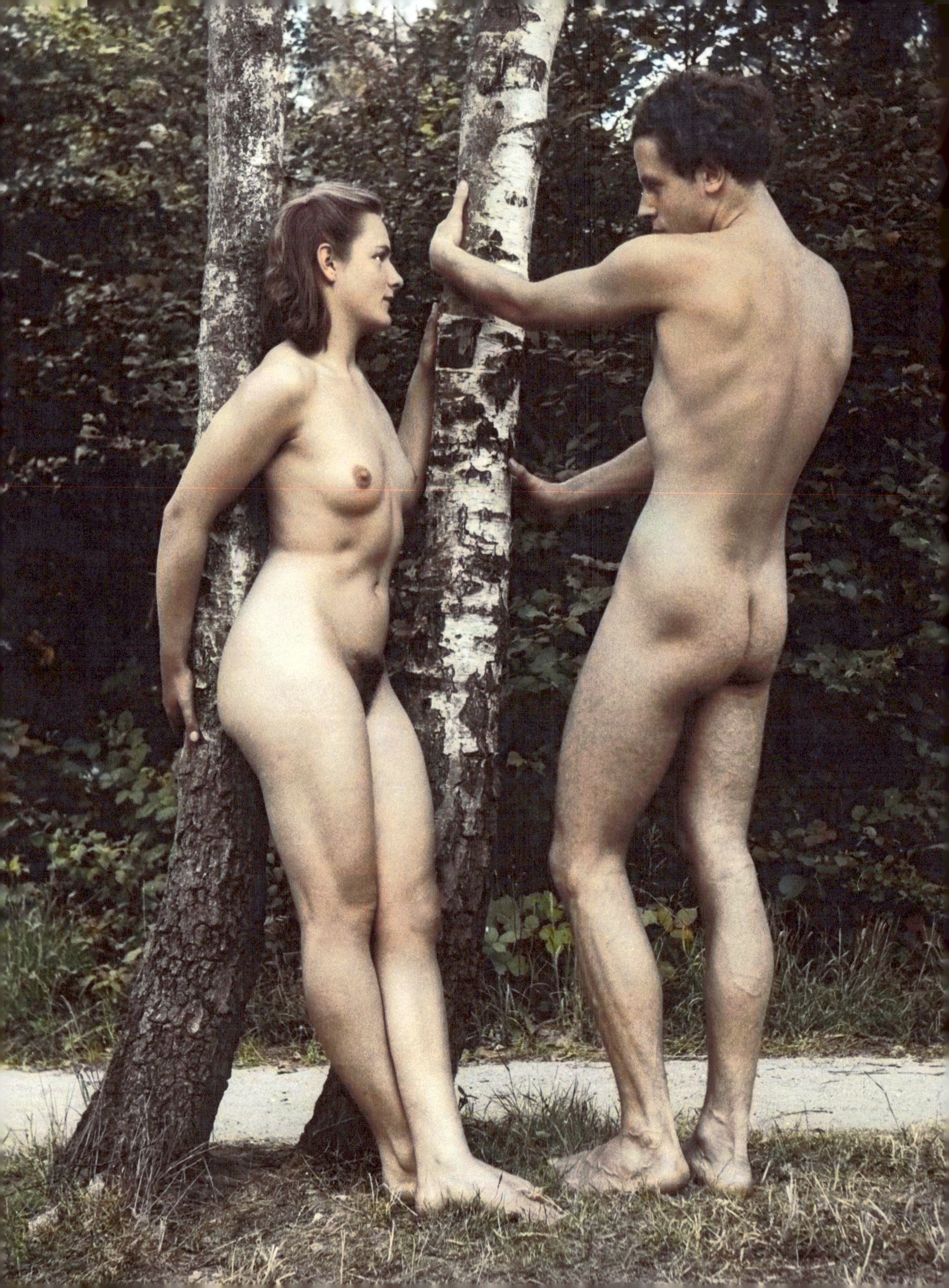

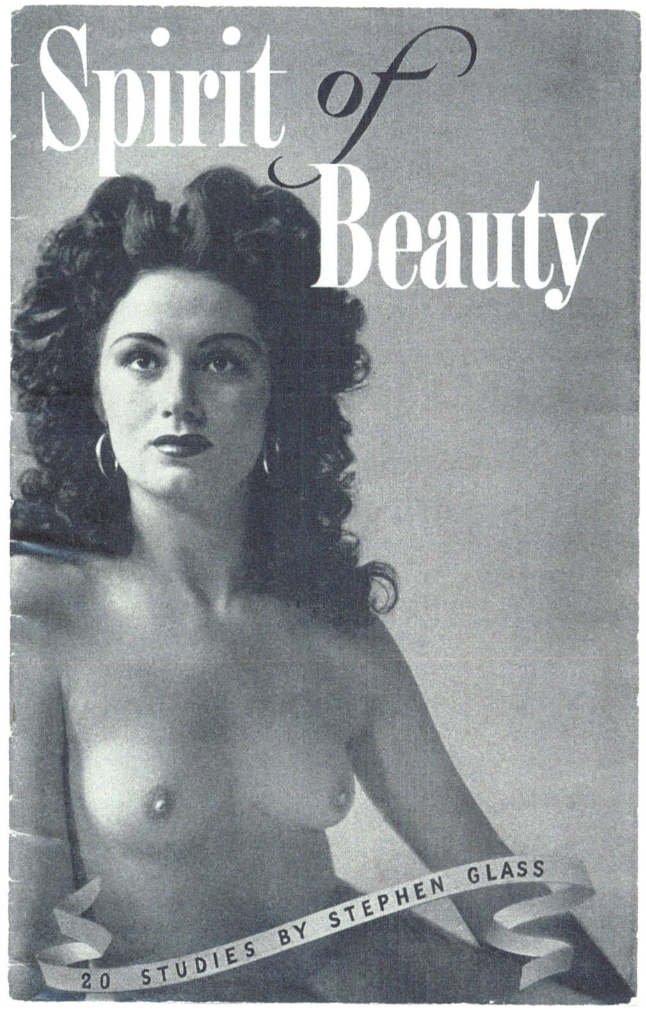

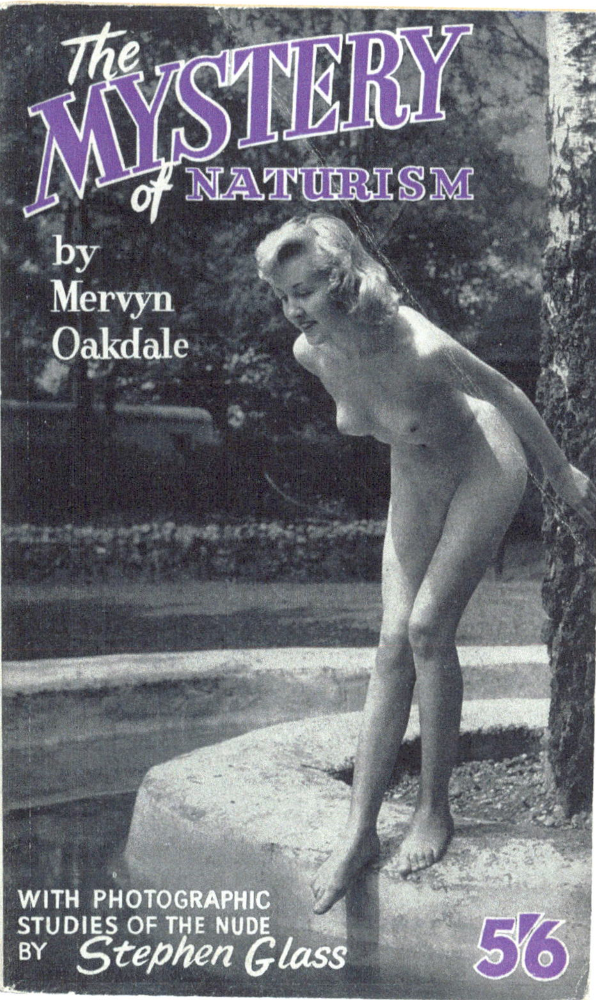

whose studio on the King's Road was enormous by comparison. Unlike Stephen, Zoltán was brisk and businesslike.

Iseult, the daughter of Spielplatz co-founders Charles and Dorothy Macaskie, remembers Stephen. "He would often ask me to pose for him," she said. "I quite enjoyed having my photo taken, but when I asked to be paid, he stopped using me. A bit of pocket money back then would have been nice."

As well as magazines, Stephen Glass's work graced a series of small books published by The Naturist Ltd., including *Sussex Maidens* (1949), *The Pool of Enchantment* (1950), and *Nudist Life in Spielplatz* (1956). He also photographed the popular model June Palmer (1940–2004). The photos in this book are from his uncensored negatives. Until the end of the 1960s, it was considered obscene

Above left: *Spirit of Beauty,* featuring 20 nude studies by Stephen Glass. A Rayburn Production, printed by Radclyffe & Company, 106 Bishopsgate, London, EC2; date unknown.

Above right: *The Mystery of Naturism* by Mervyn Oakdale, with photographic studies of the nude by Stephen Glass. Published by The Naturist Ltd., 222 Gray's Inn Road, London WC1; 1941.

to show pubic hair or genitalia in British publications. To ensure that an image of a naked young lady would not incur the censor's wrath, the model would shave down below, and the photograph would then be retouched by hand to erase anything problematic.

By 1964, Zoltán Glass had made enough money to sell his Chelsea studios to a consortium of British photographers. He then moved to a villa in Roquebrune on the French Riviera with his common-law wife Pat, a former cabaret dancer. He offered his collection of pin-up photography to glamour photographer Harrison Marks who, strangely, turned it down. Zoltán died in France on February 24, 1981, at the age of 78, leaving neither offspring nor a will. His photographs were eventually given to The National Science and Media Museum in Bradford, Yorkshire. Stephen Glass died on April 23, 1990. His work ended up at auction.

Right: Jean Cobb

Below: Magazine advert from 1952 for the new edition of *British Naturism,* featuring a photographic supplement of nude studies by Stephen Glass.

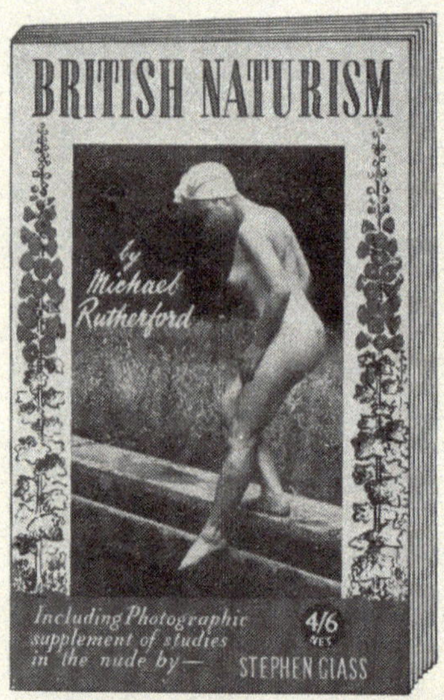

Completely Up to Date !

THE *NEW EDITION* OF

'BRITISH NATURISM'

The Most Important Book on Social Nudism Ever Written: Photographs of Nudist Clubs; Facts; Anecdotes; Descriptions; Revelations

The brilliant cover is printed in three colours and there are pages of outstanding photographs by Stephen Glass. The book is obtainable from all newsagents or direct by post from The Naturist (1941) Ltd., 222-224, Gray's Inn Road, London, W.C.1.

4/6 NET By Post 5/-

MAKE SURE OF YOUR COPY TODAY

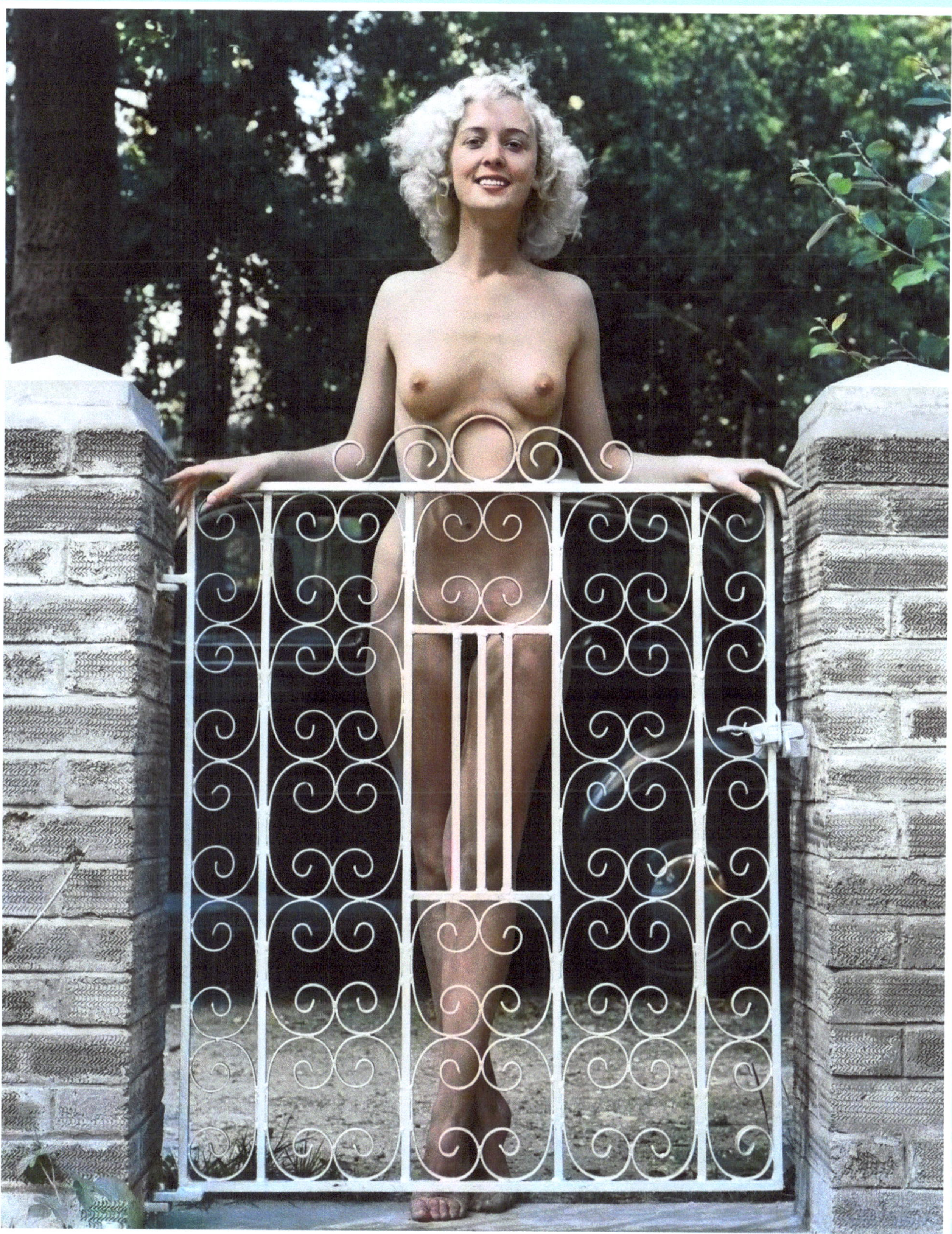

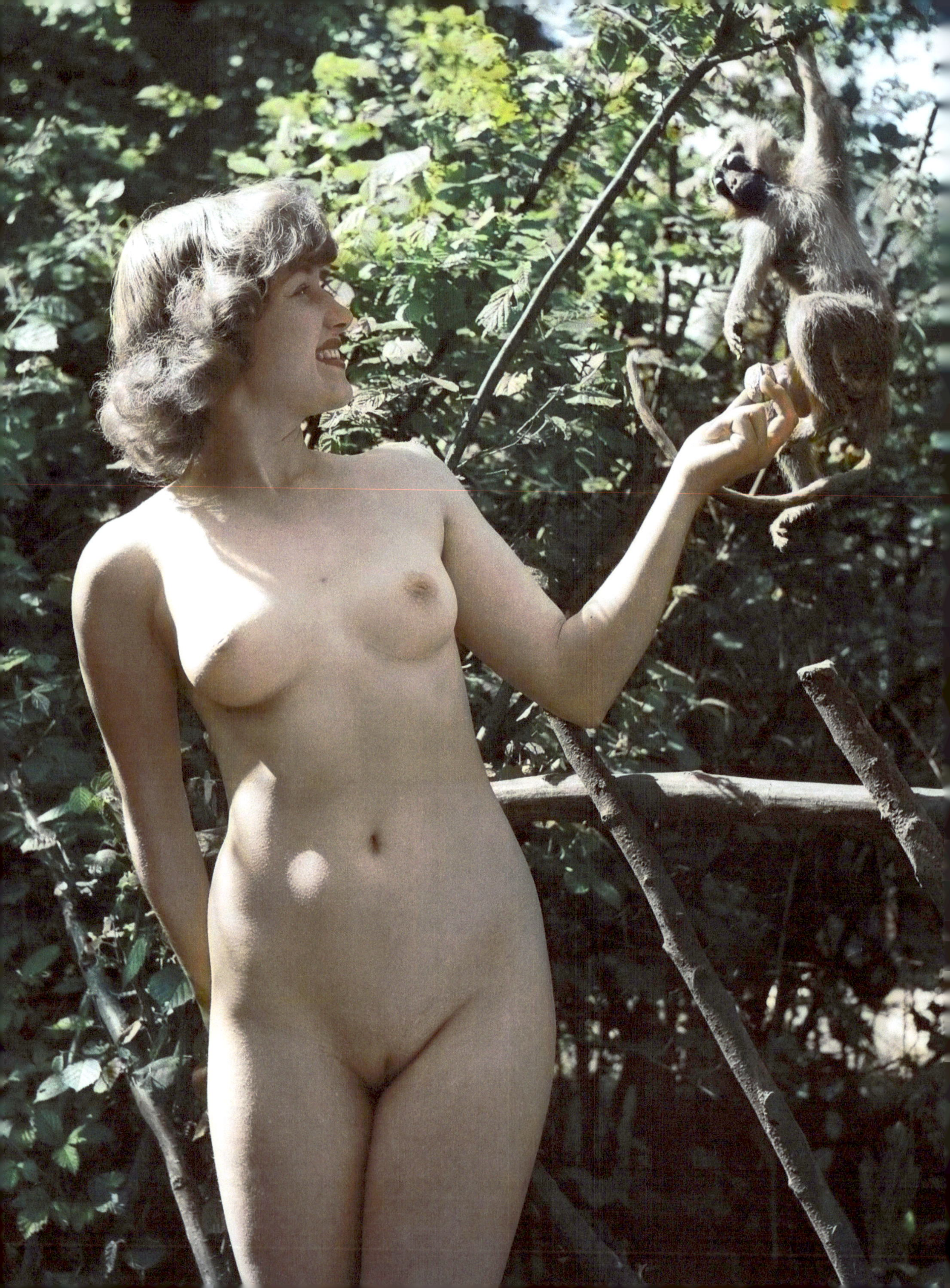

When designing the covers for the William Welby books *Naked and Unashamed,* *The Naked Truth about Nudism,* and *It's Only Natural,* I colourized some black-and-white photographs by Stephen Glass. The results exceeded my expectations and led me to consider publishing an additional volume in the Stephen Glass Collection featuring colourized images. This book is the result.

The process of colourization begins with scanning the original black-and-white photographs at high resolution, from a print or a negative. High-resolution scans ensure that all the fine details are captured. Once scanned, the images undergo cleanup to remove dust, scratches, and other imperfections that have accumulated over the years. Next comes the colourization process, which requires careful attention to detail to ensure that the colours look natural and true to the period – a delicate dance between artistry and authenticity. Not all black-and-white images are suitable for colourization. Some photographs are better left in black and white, especially if they were carefully designed and conceived as such.

In the pages that follow, you'll find a curated selection of Stephen Glass's photographs that I have colourized for your viewing pleasure. I sincerely hope this allows you to deepen your appreciation of his work as you rediscover it through a vibrant new lens. Enjoy.

— B. Fotherington-Tomas

Below: Before and after – a black-and-white image that was colourized.

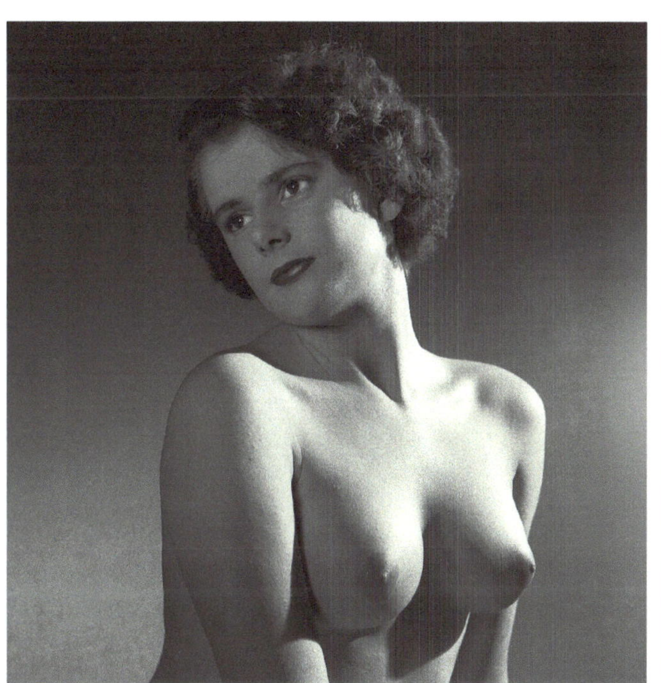

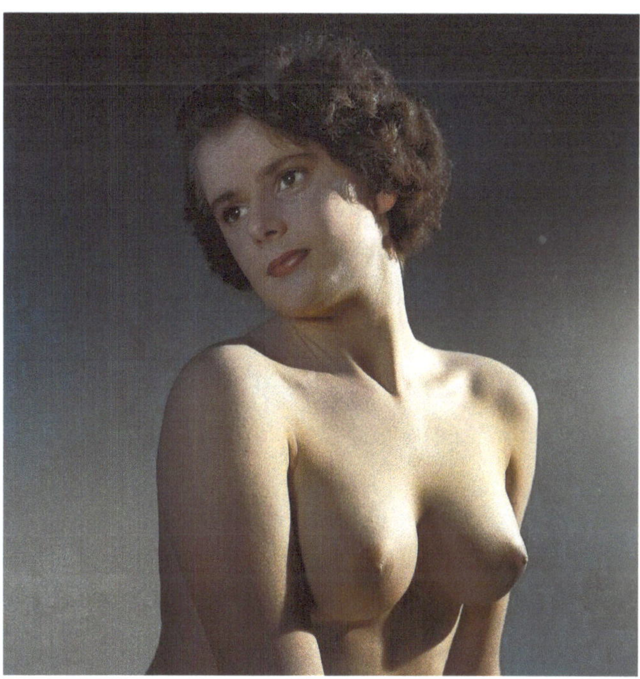

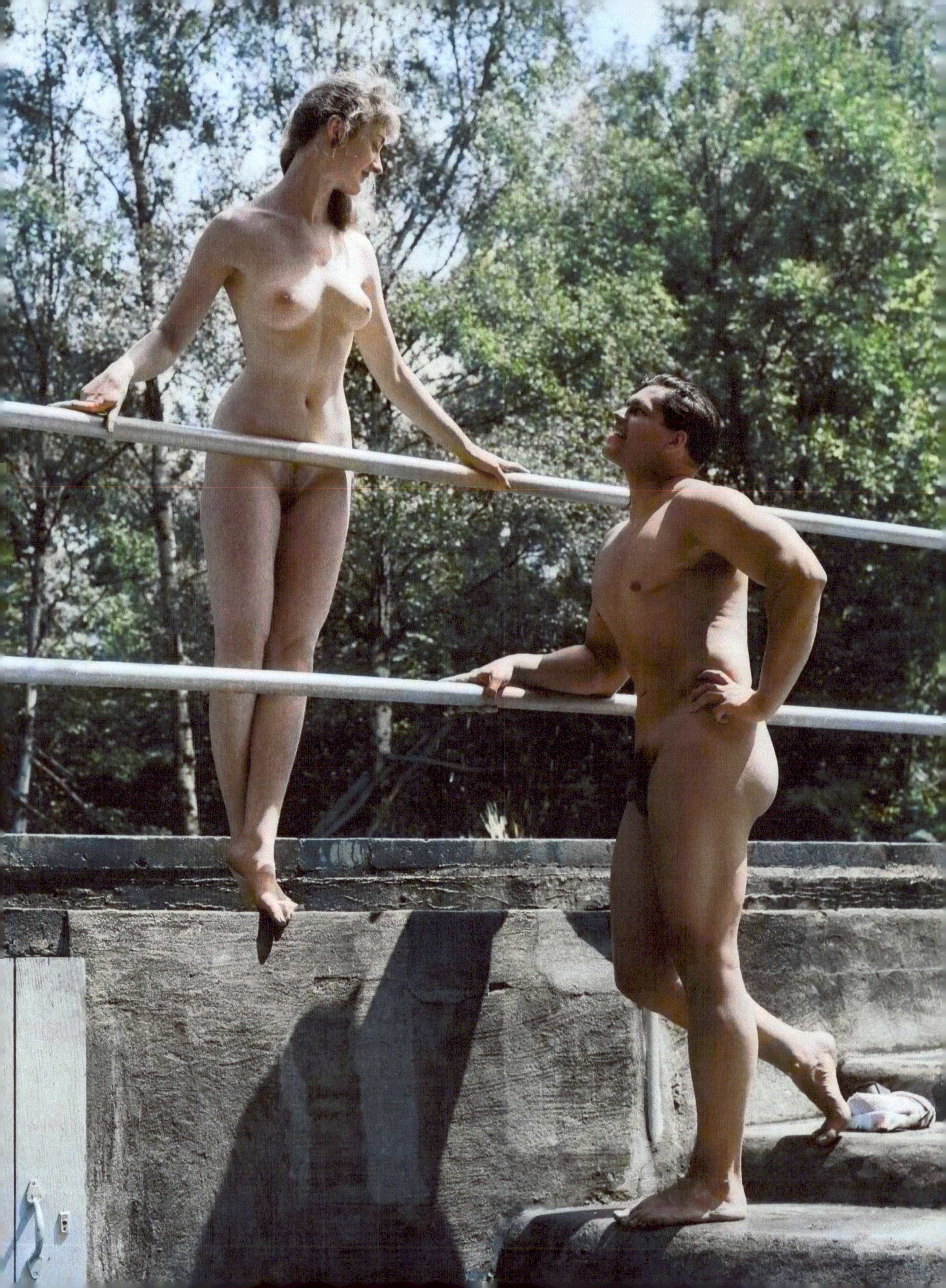

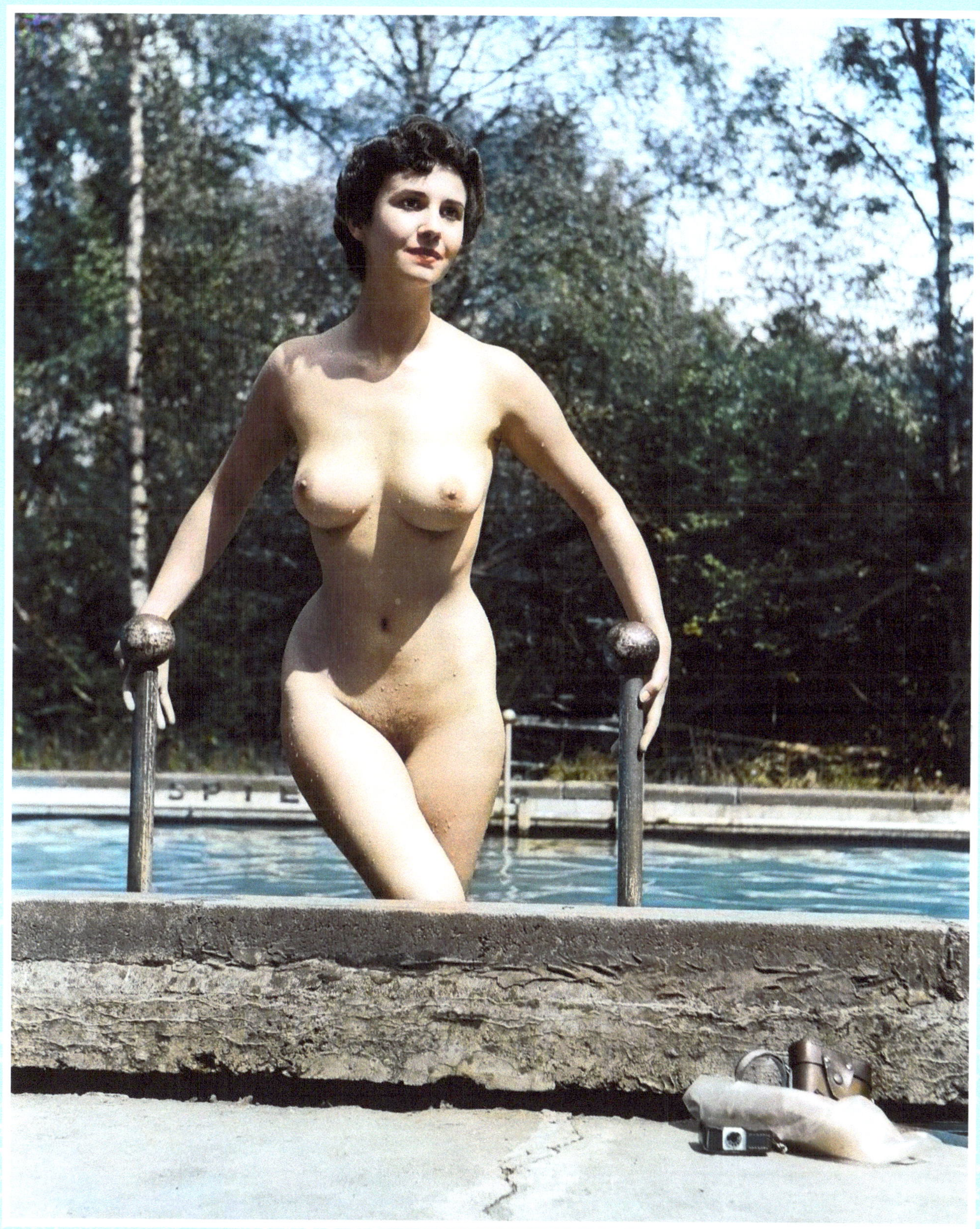

Above: Anita Smith at the pool at Spielplatz nudist village, St Albans.

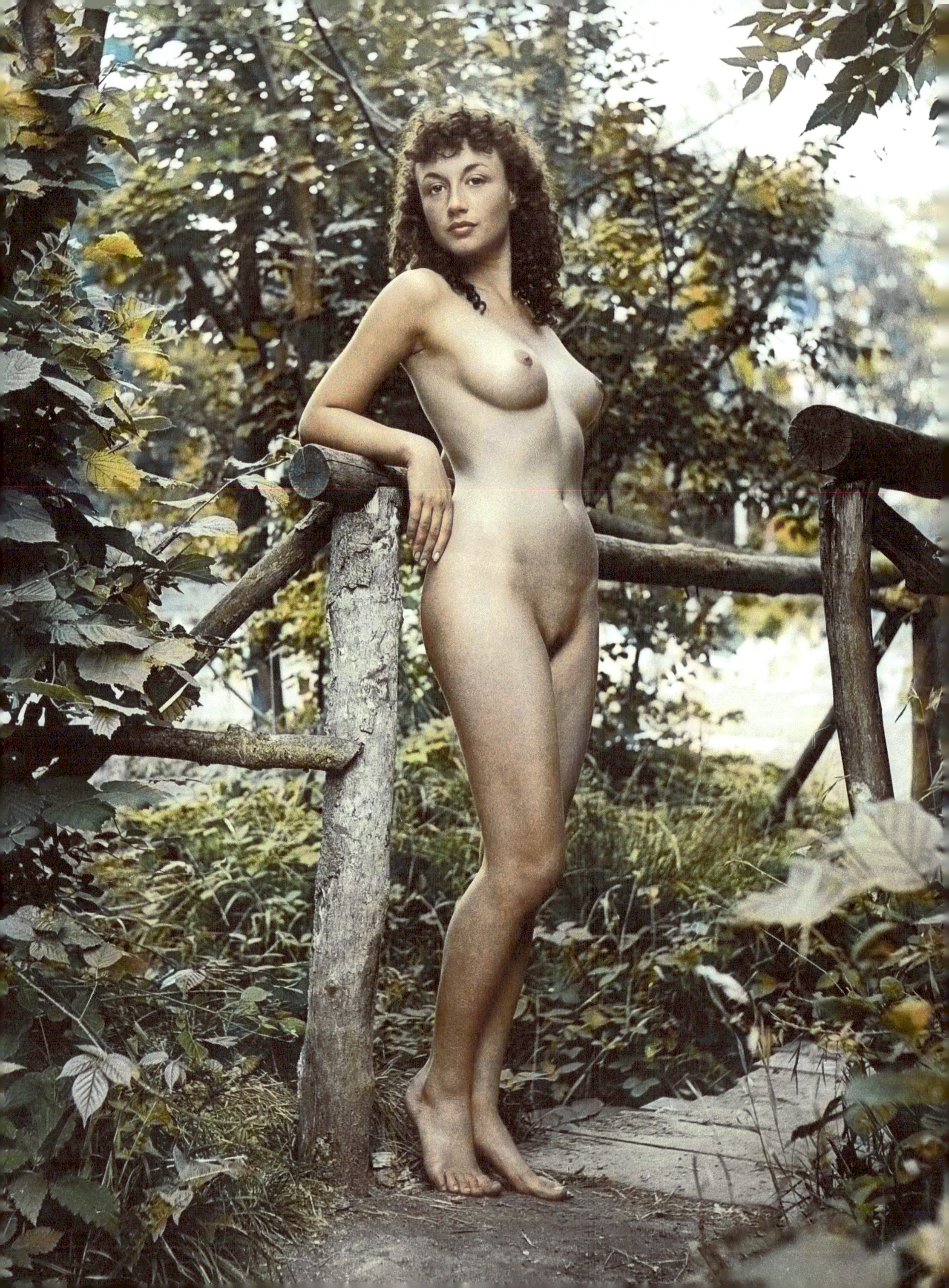

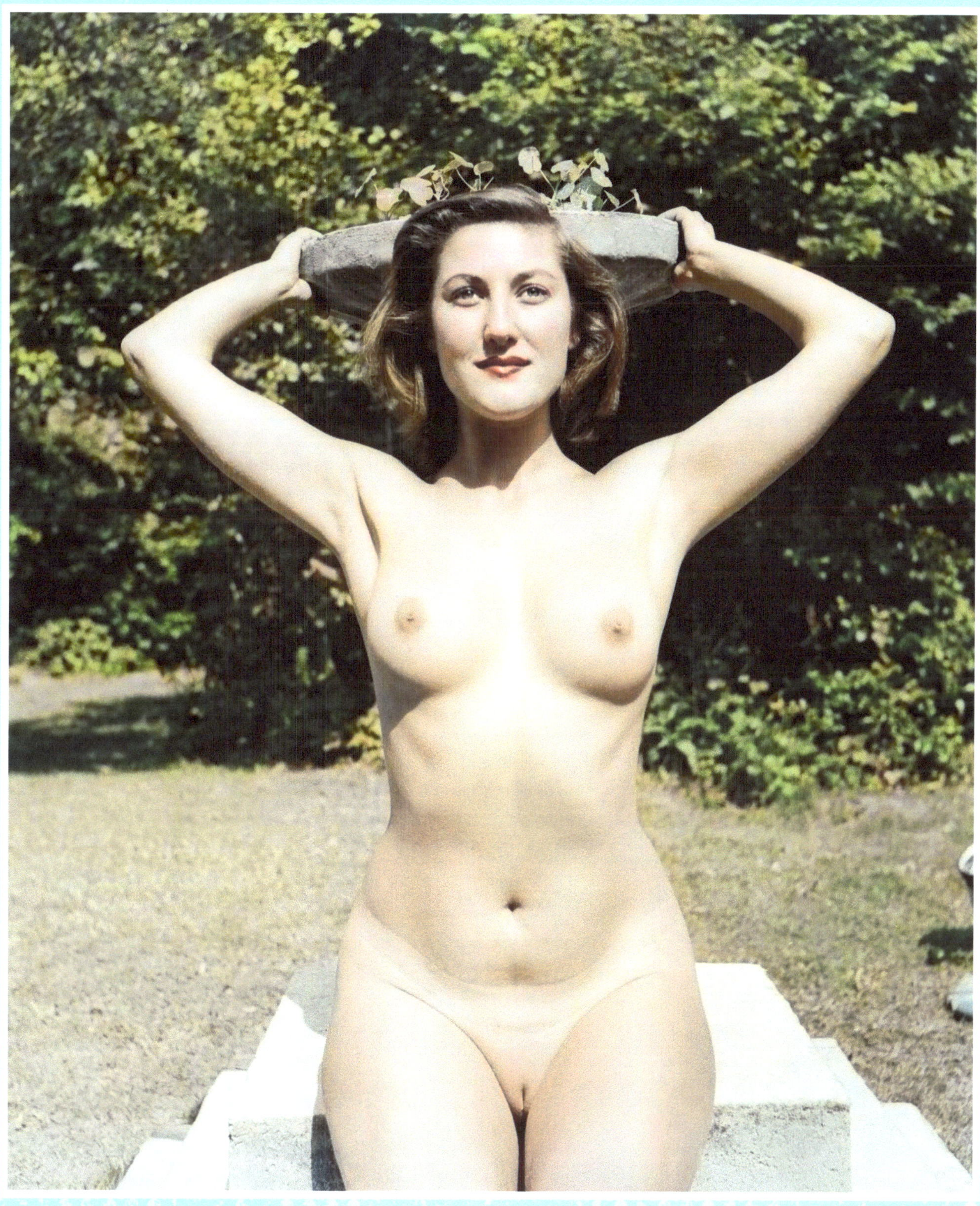

Above: Barbara Thourgood. **Left:** Pamela Green, photographed in the grounds of Spielplatz, St Albans. The image featured in *Health and Efficiency* magazine in January 1951 with the title "Resting Dancer".

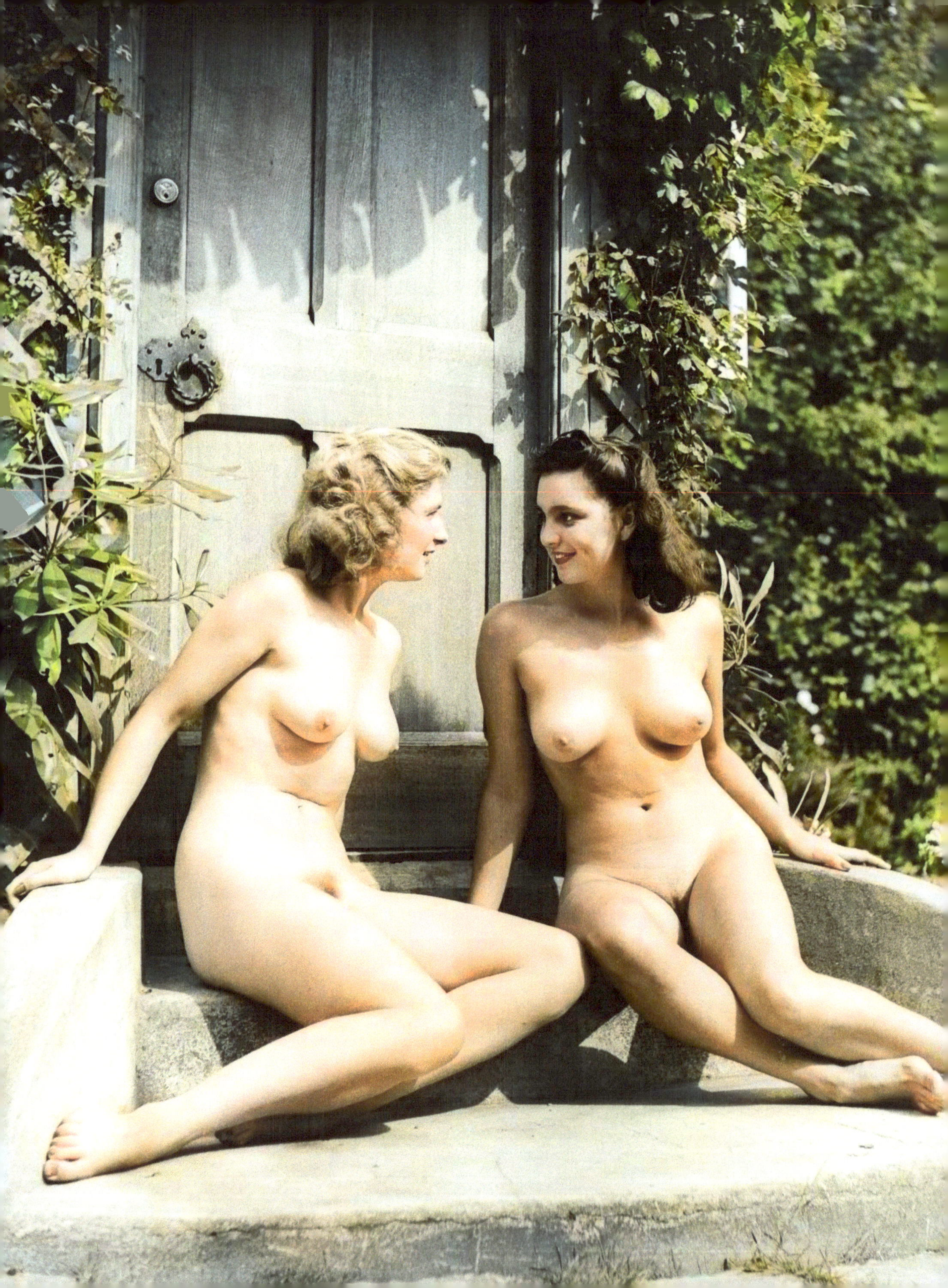

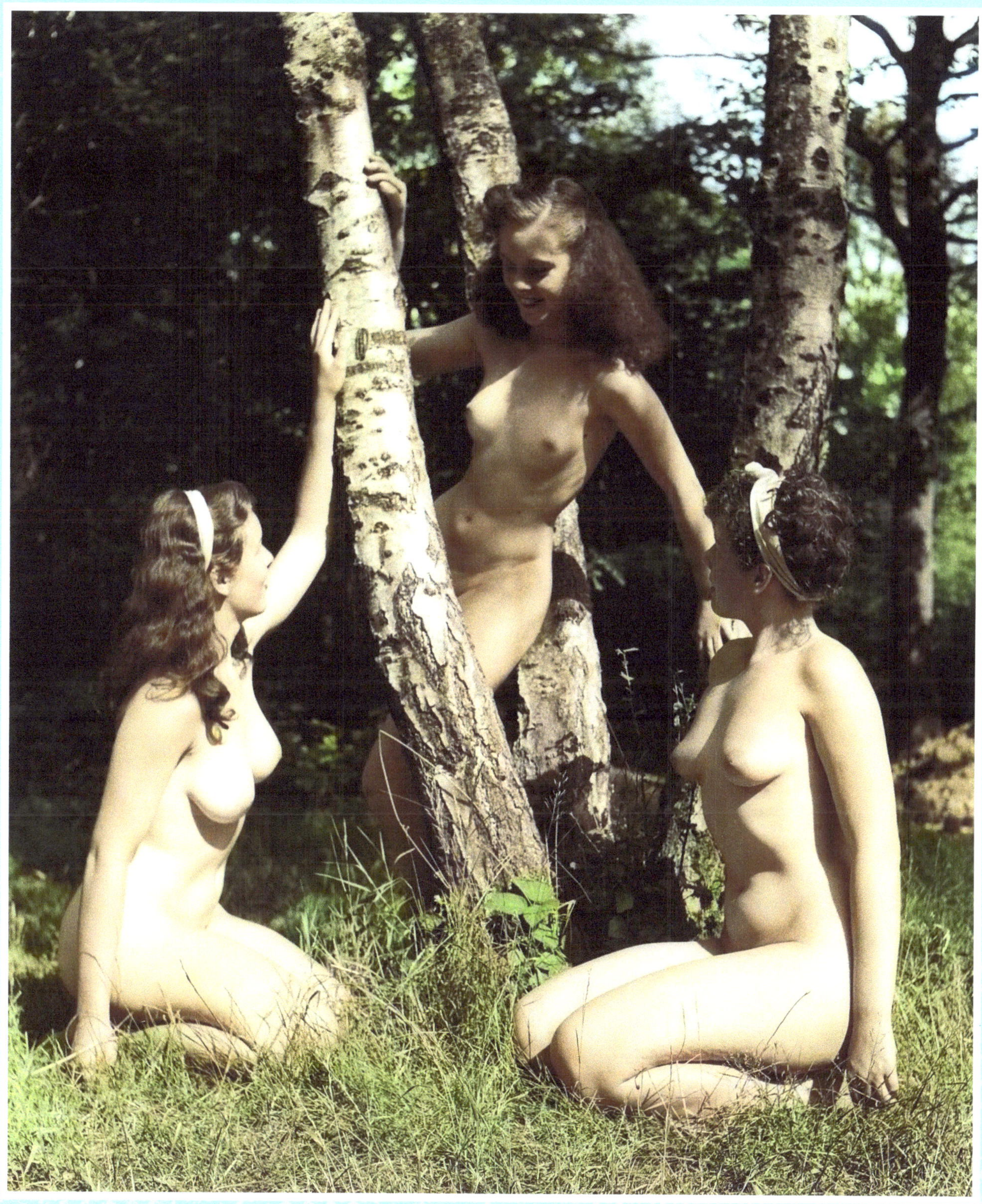

Above centre: Mina Maureen Liberoff (1931–2016), née Felgate. **Left:** Audrey Goodman and Beryl Sidey.

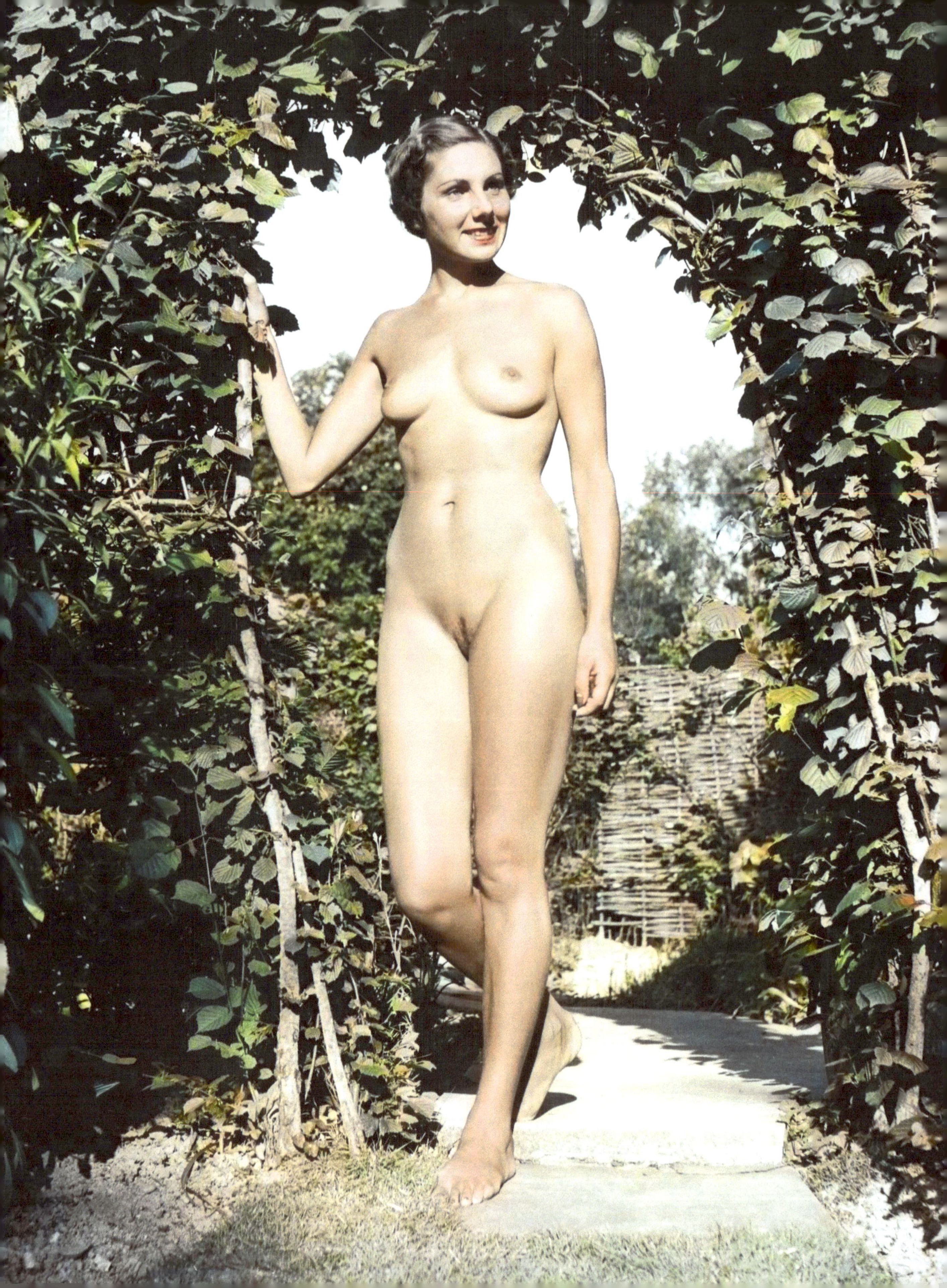

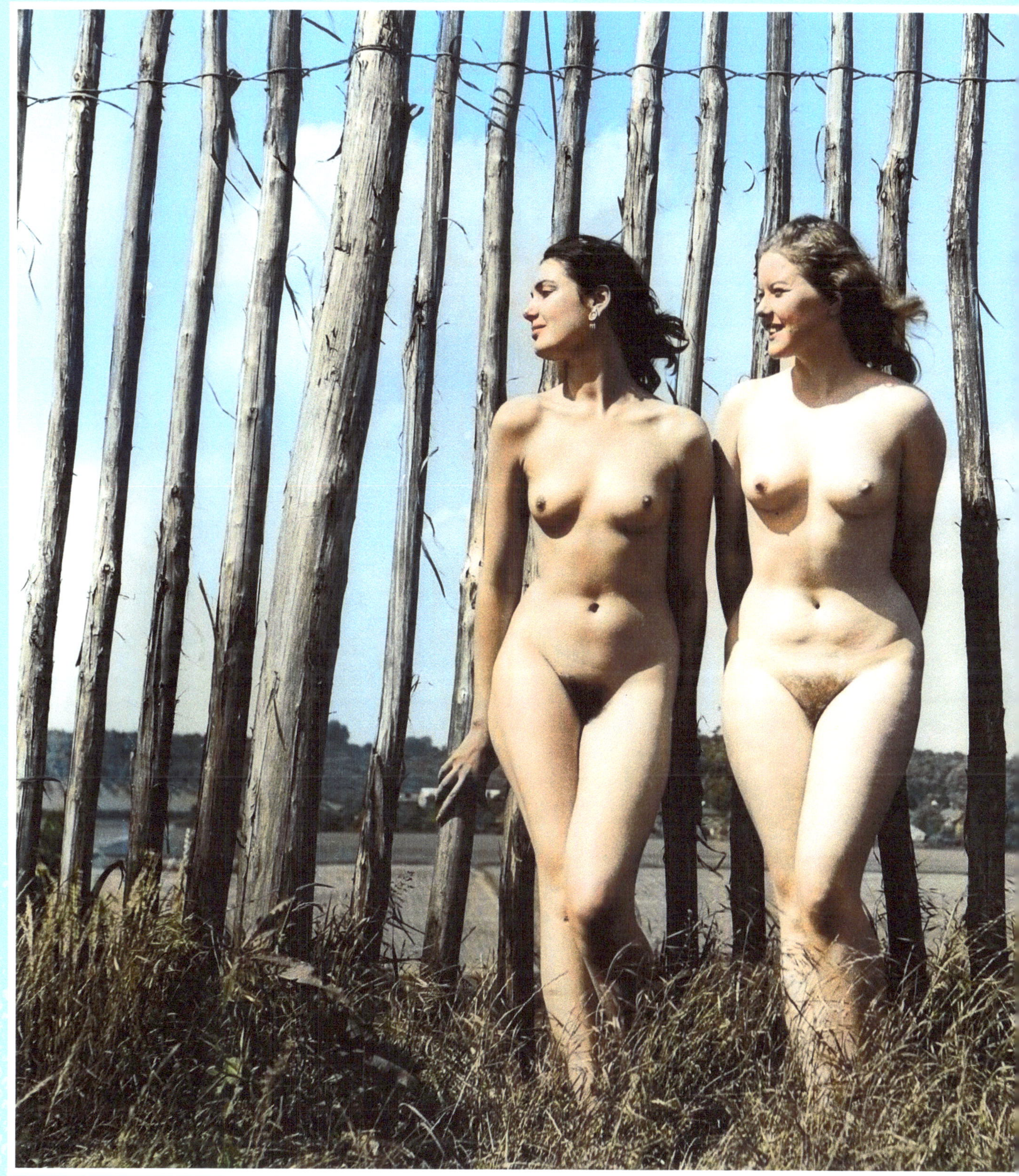

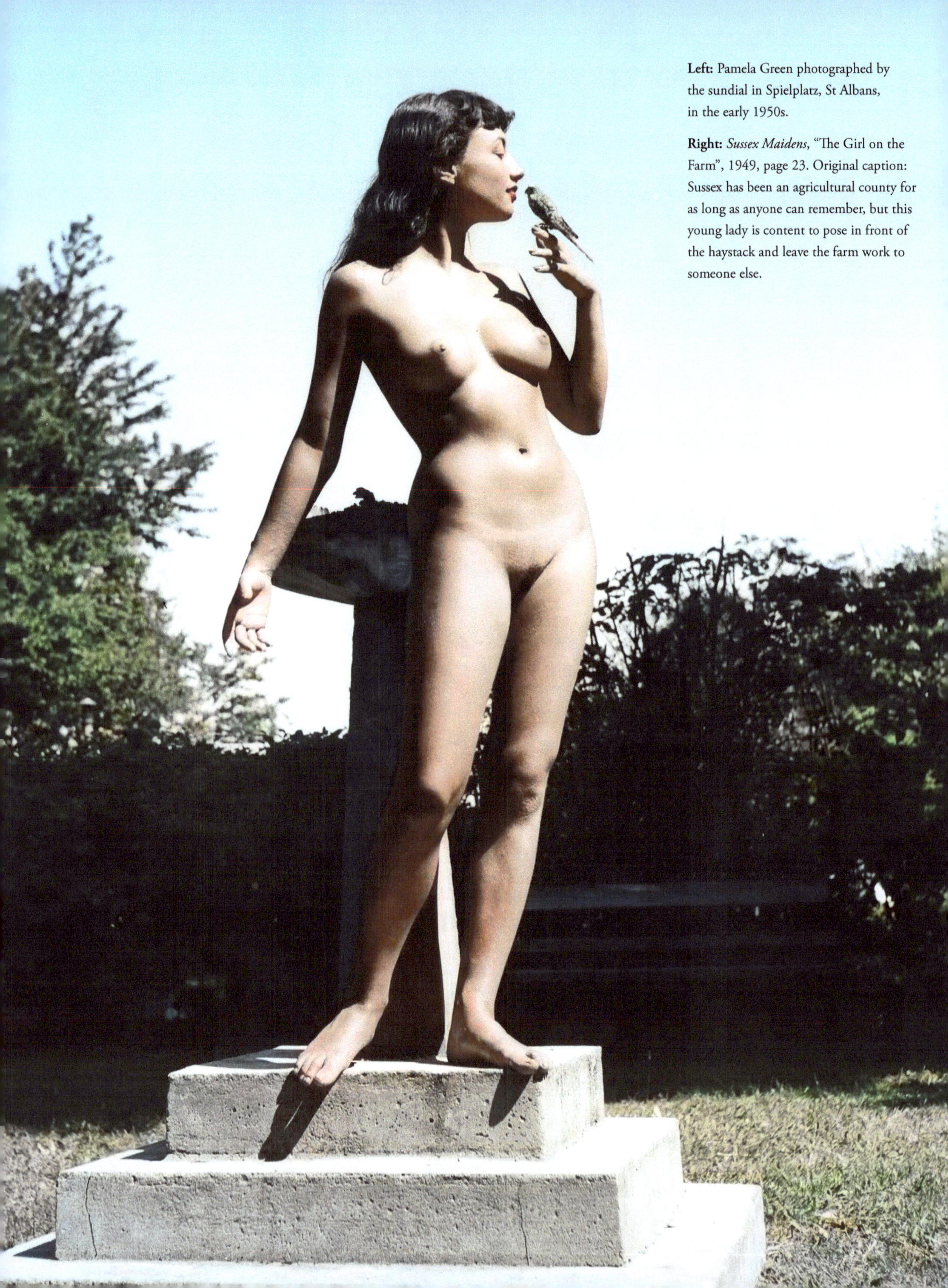

Left: Pamela Green photographed by
the sundial in Spielplatz, St Albans,
in the early 1950s.

Right: *Sussex Maidens*, "The Girl on the
Farm", 1949, page 23. Original caption:
Sussex has been an agricultural county for
as long as anyone can remember, but this
young lady is content to pose in front of
the haystack and leave the farm work to
someone else.

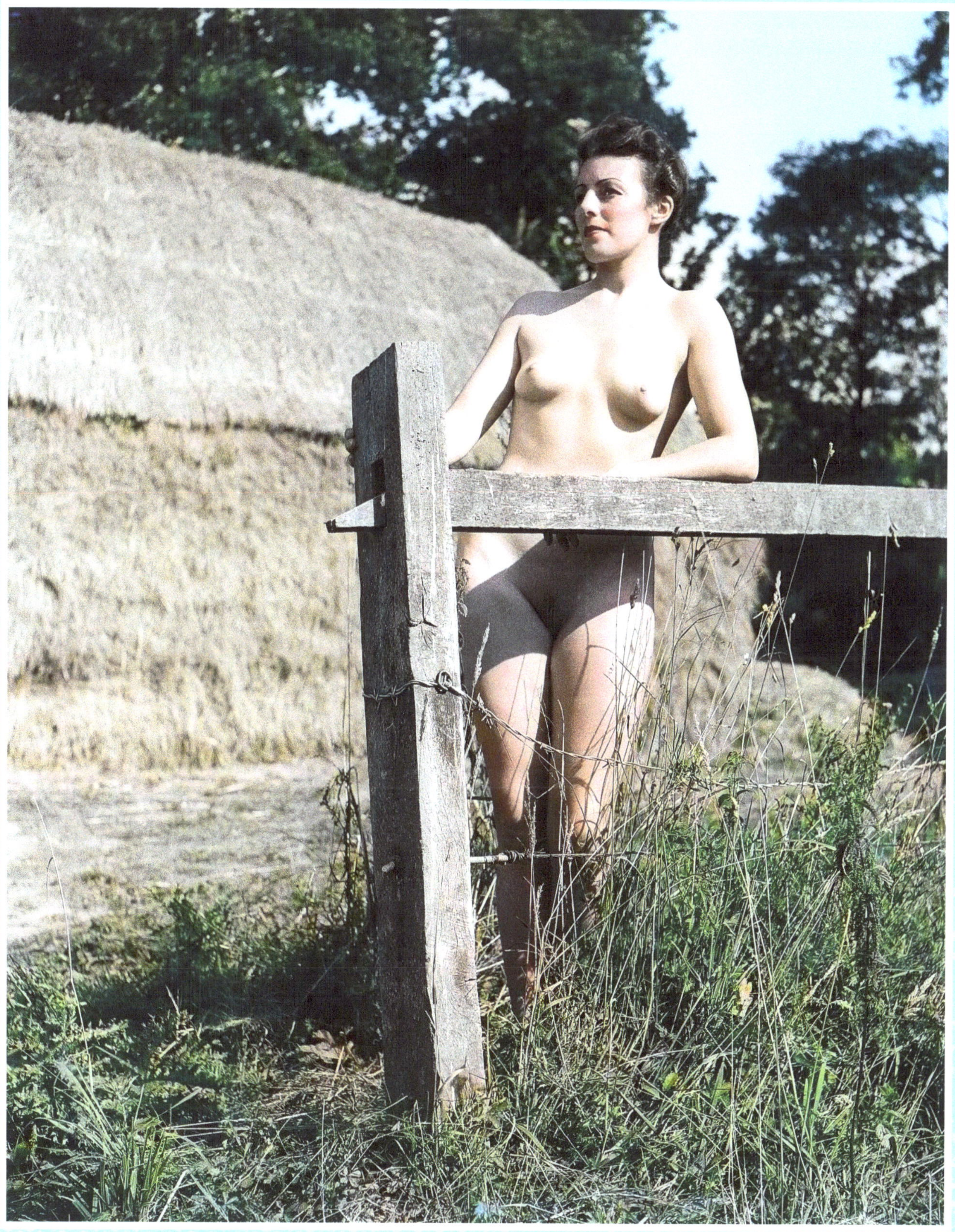

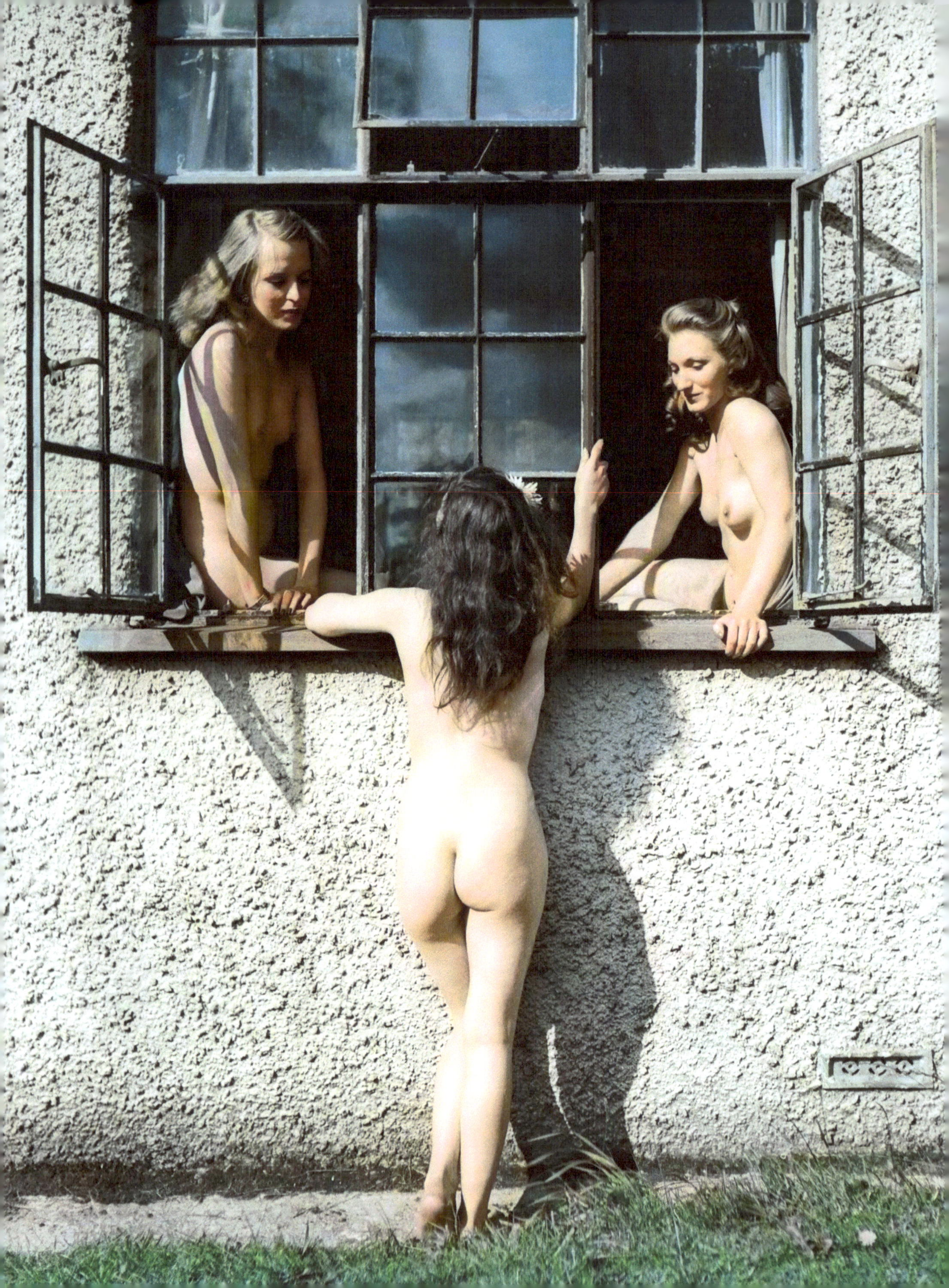

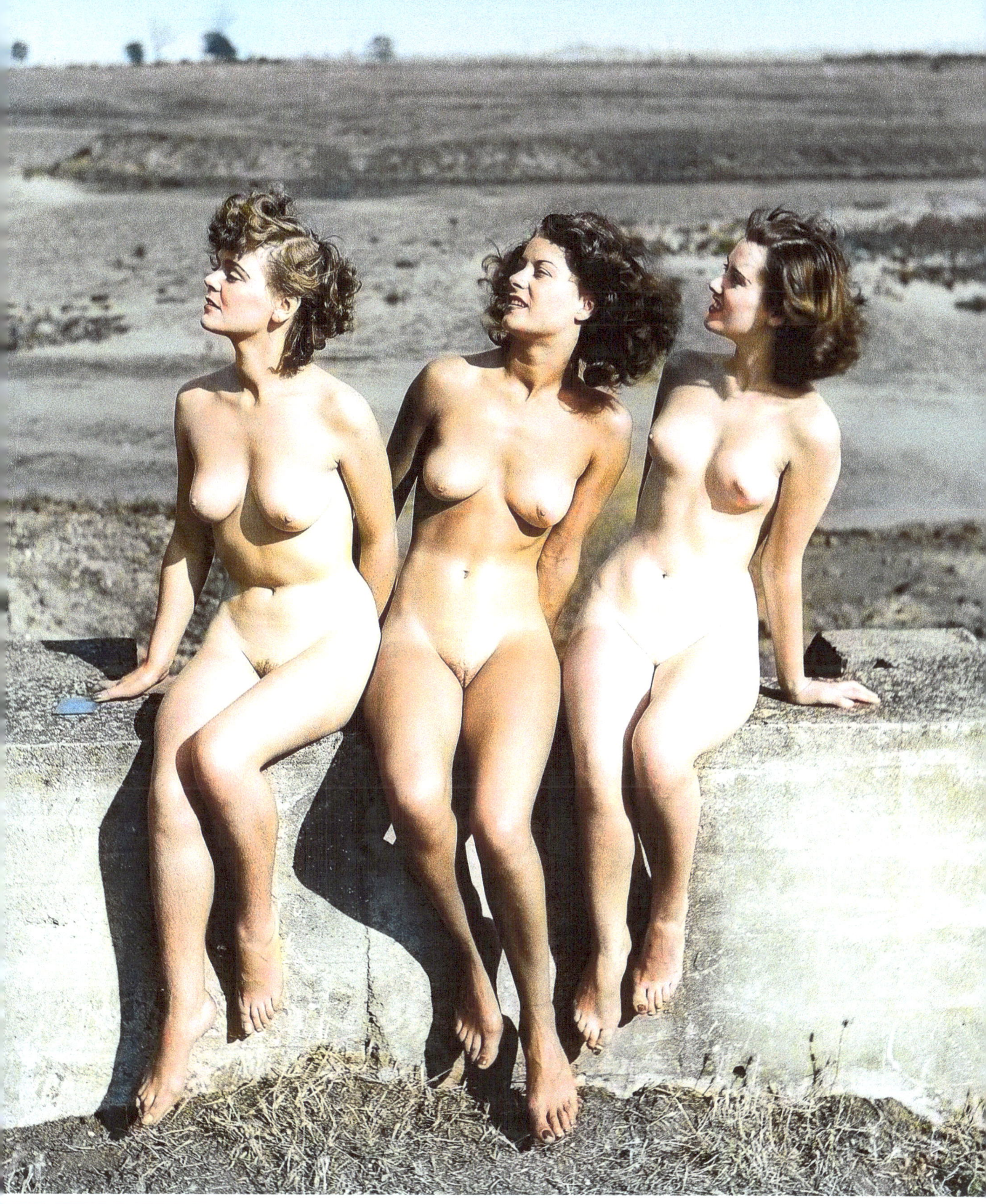

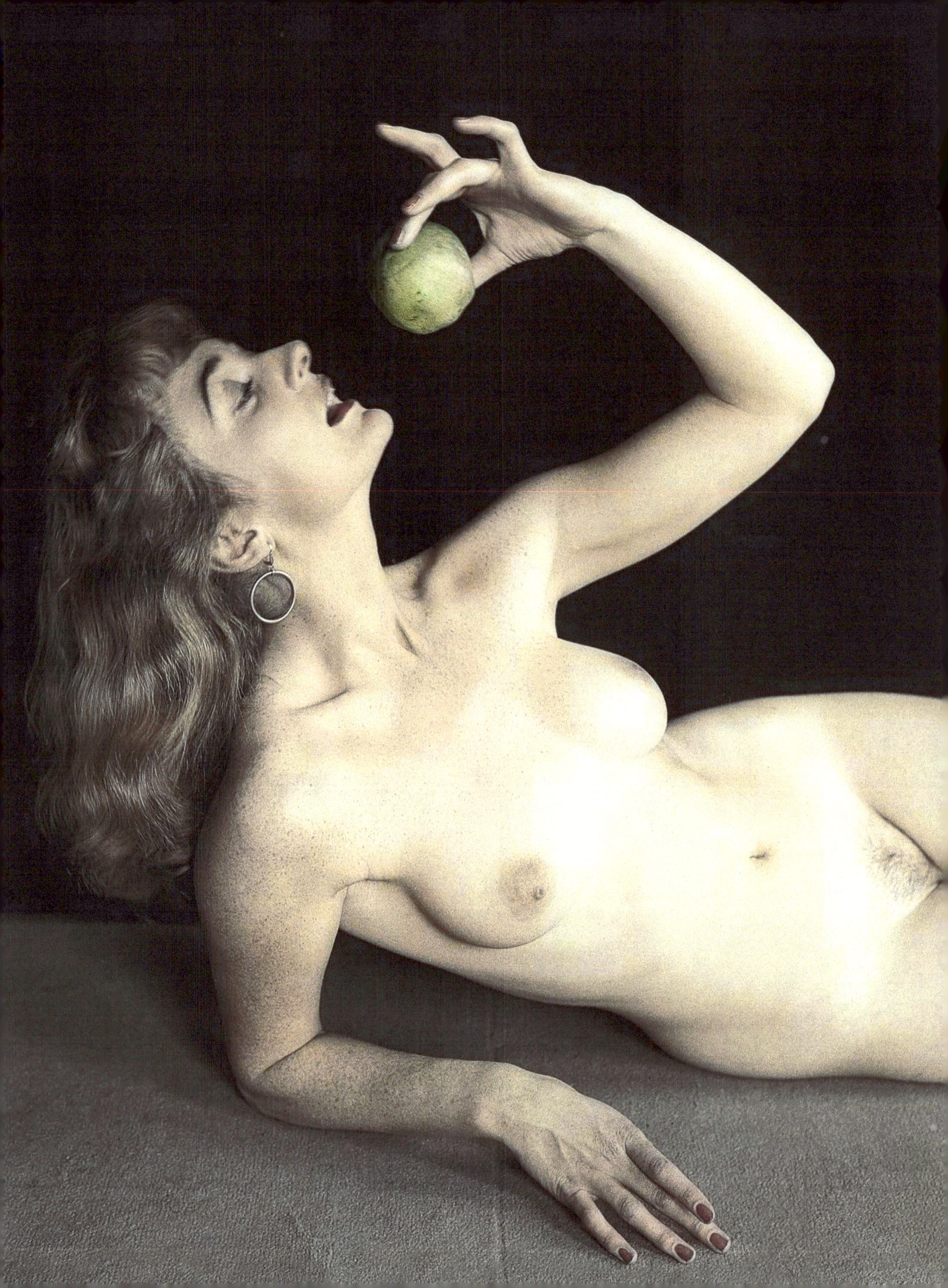

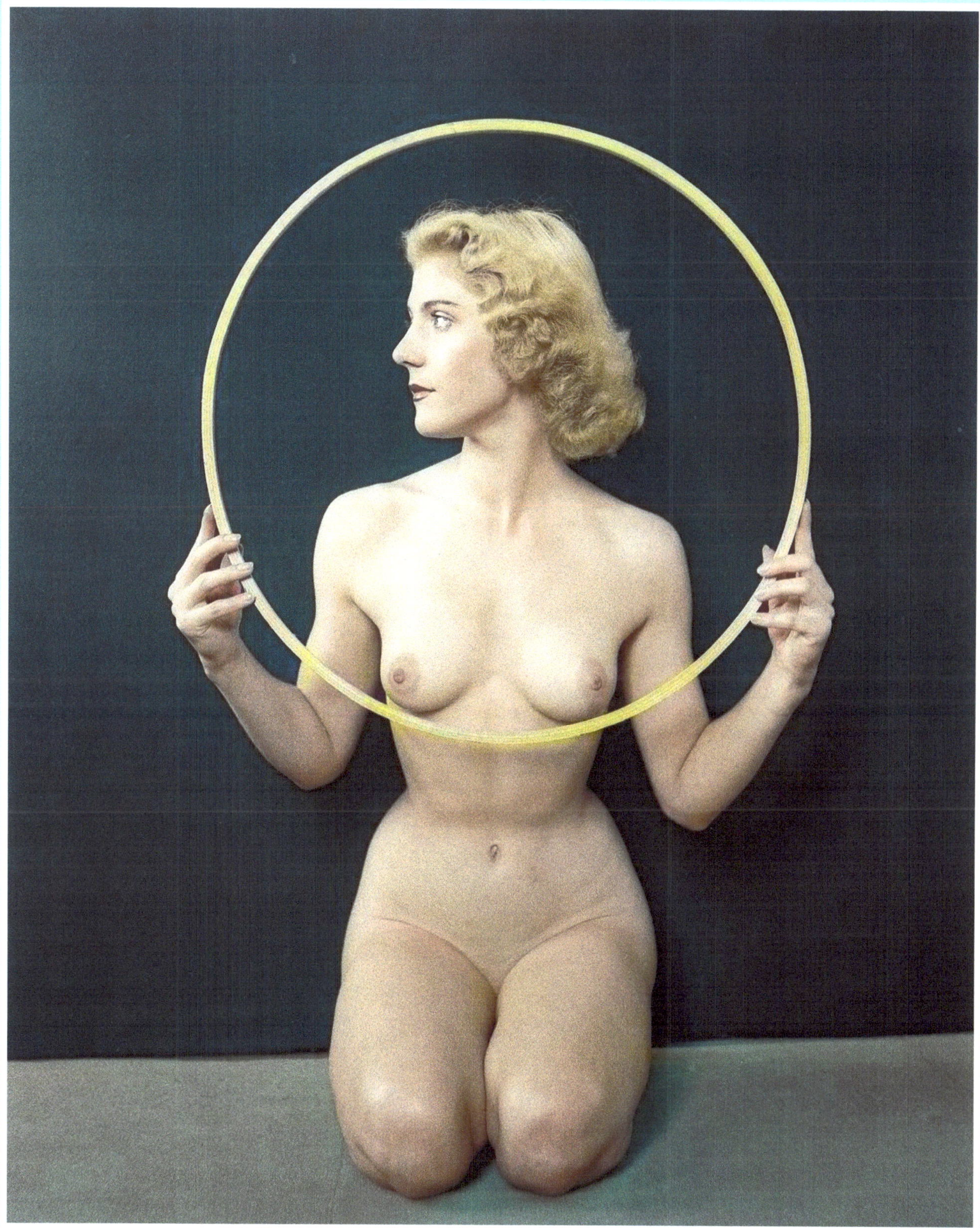

Left: Eve Harrison

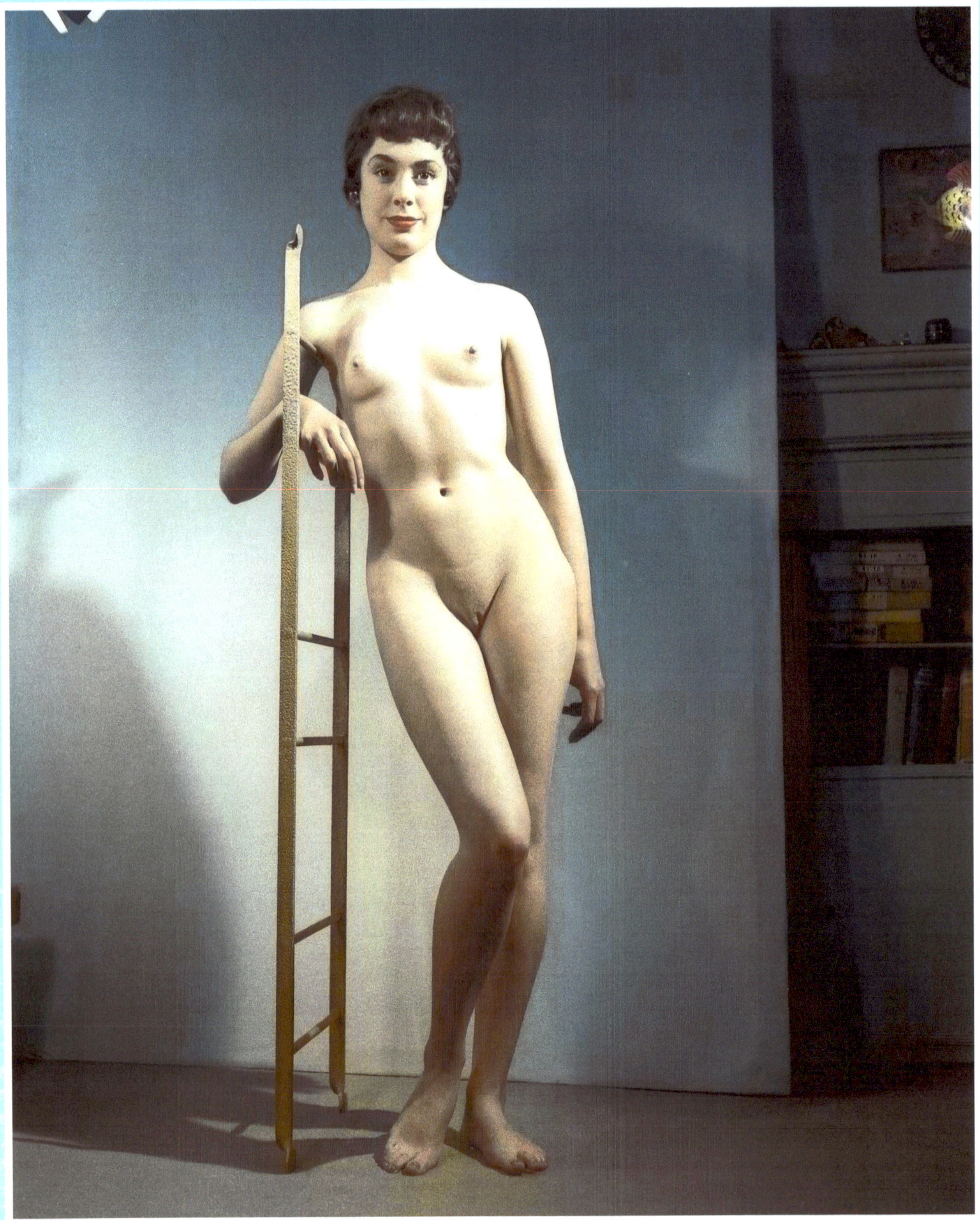

Above: Mara Fox.

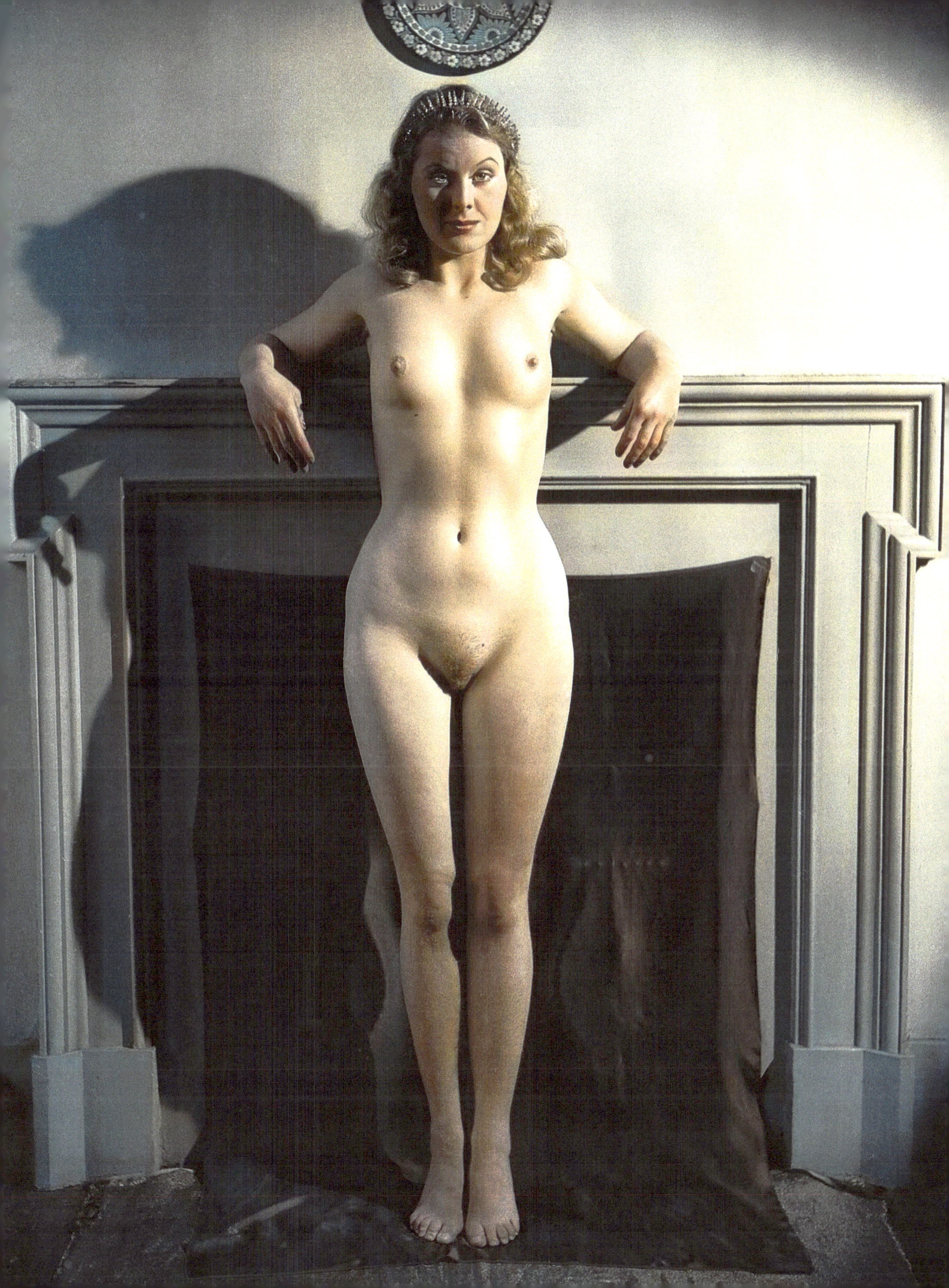

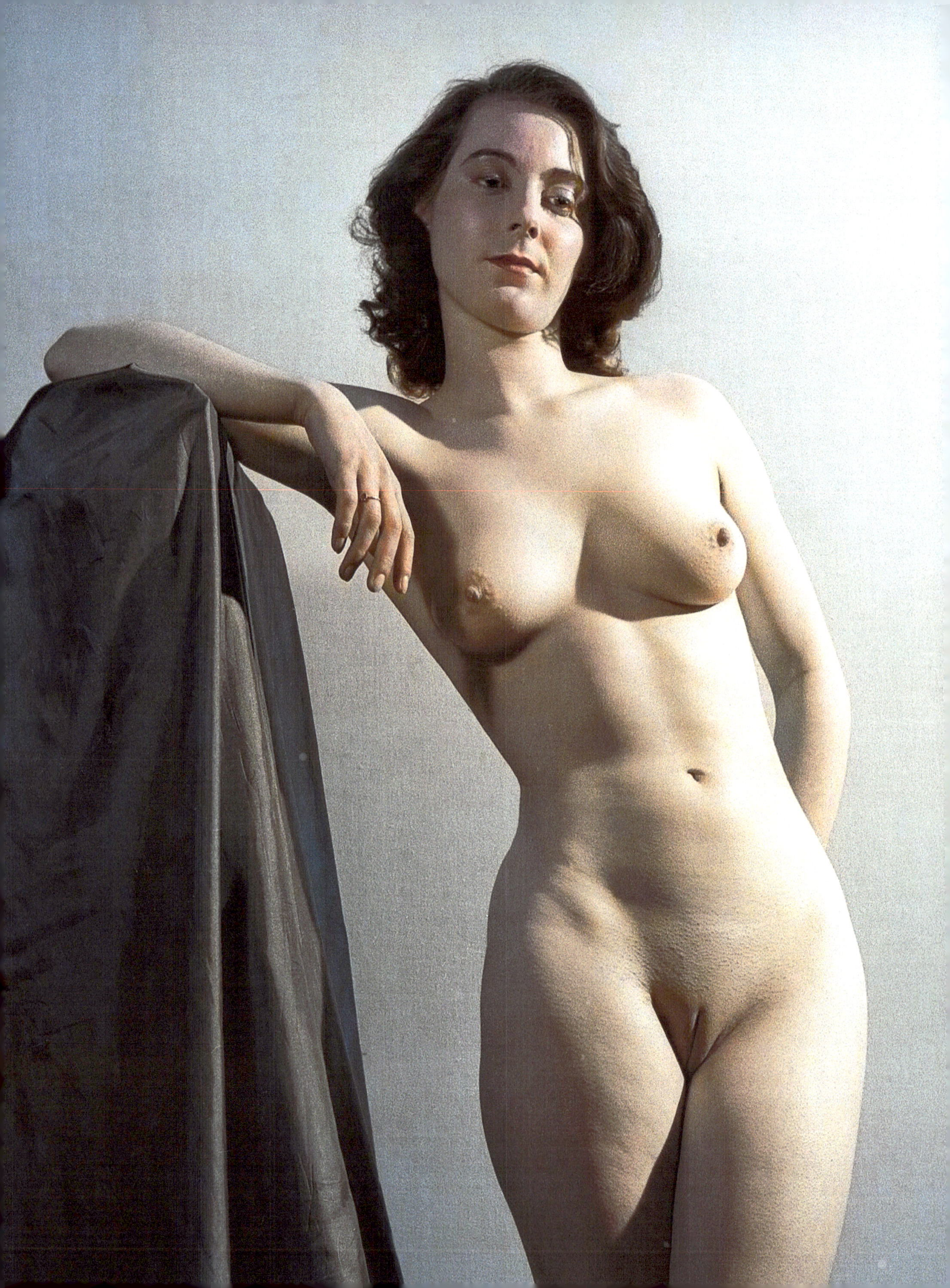

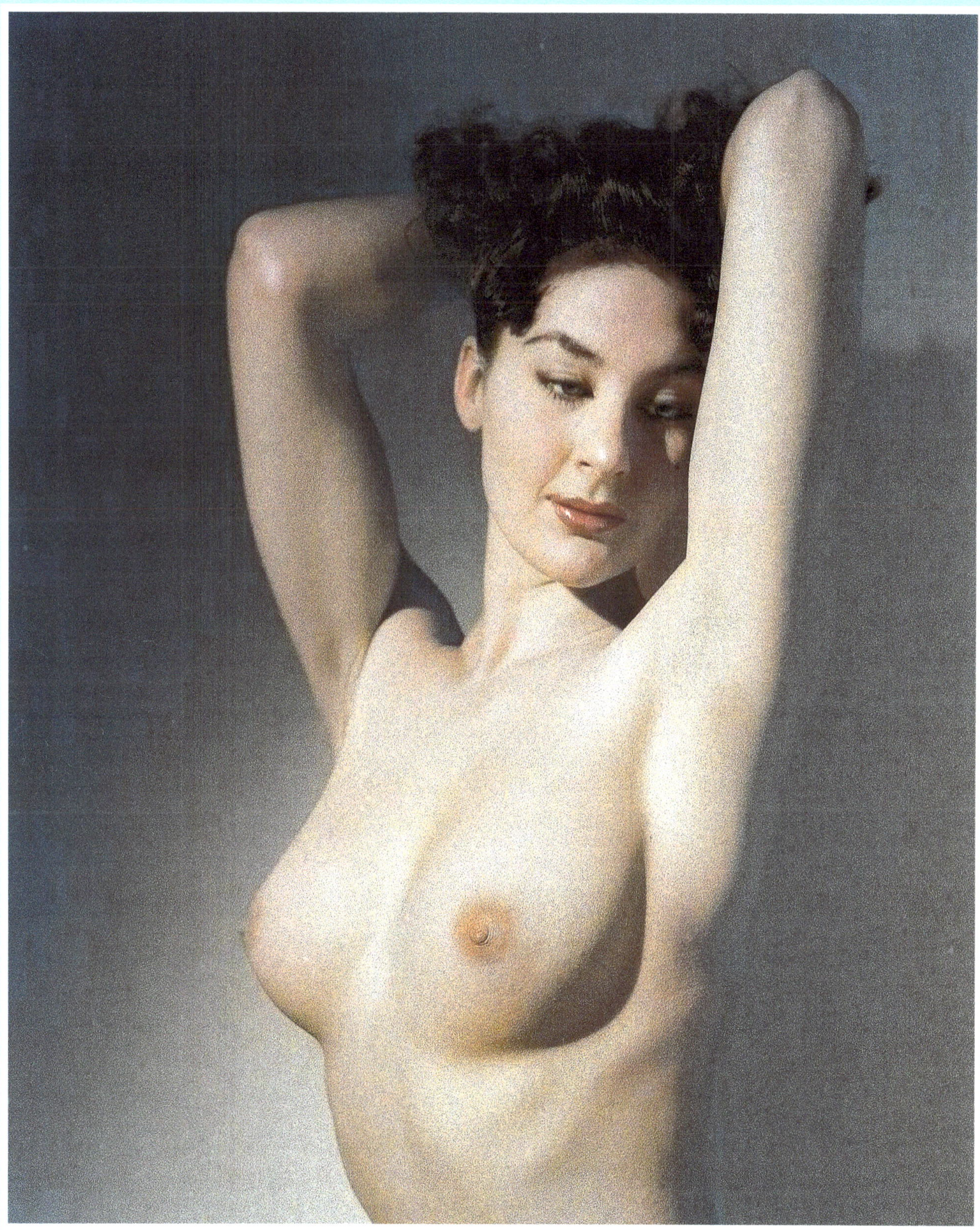

Above: Lee Sothern (aka Grace Jackson).

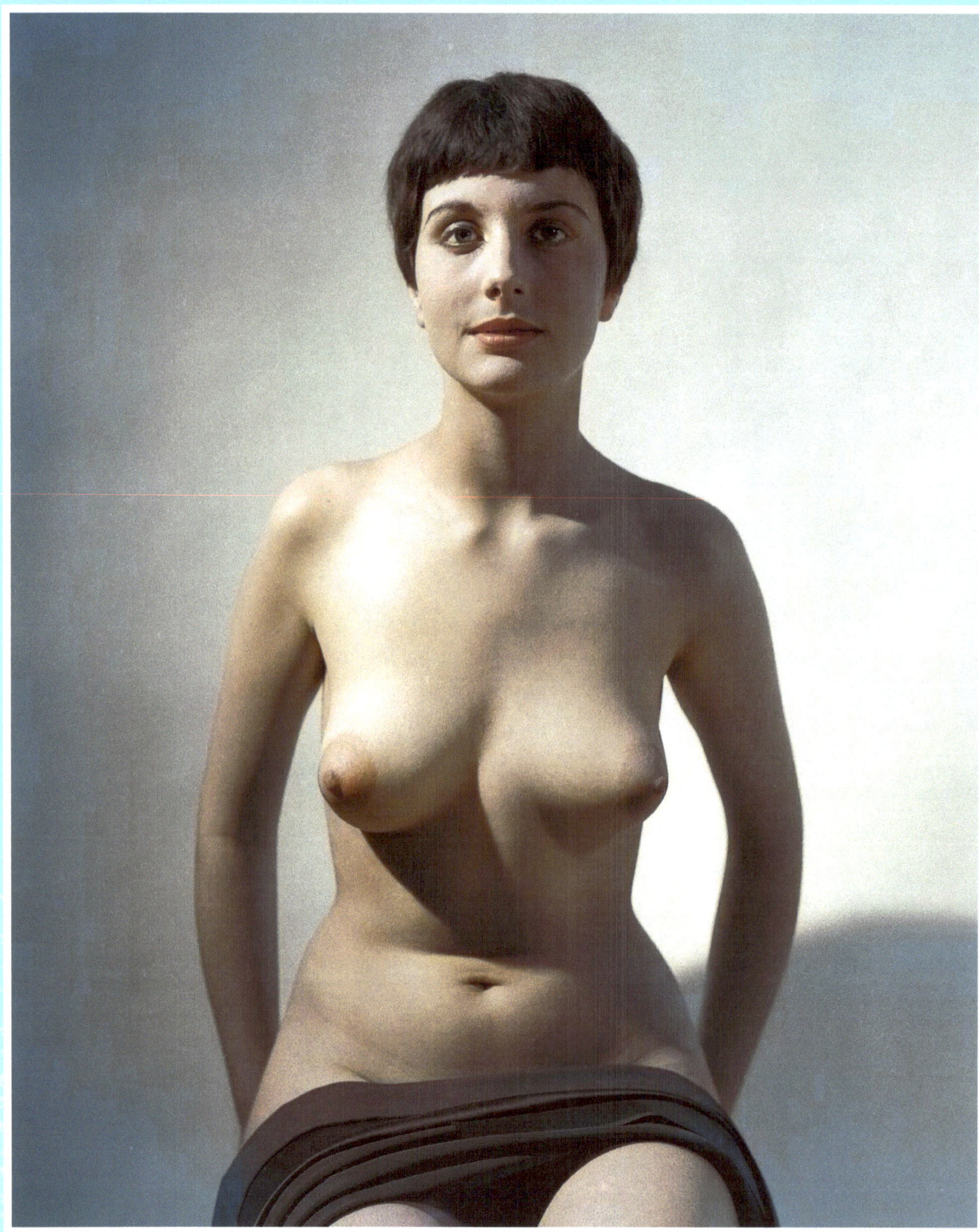

Above: Susan Rothwell.

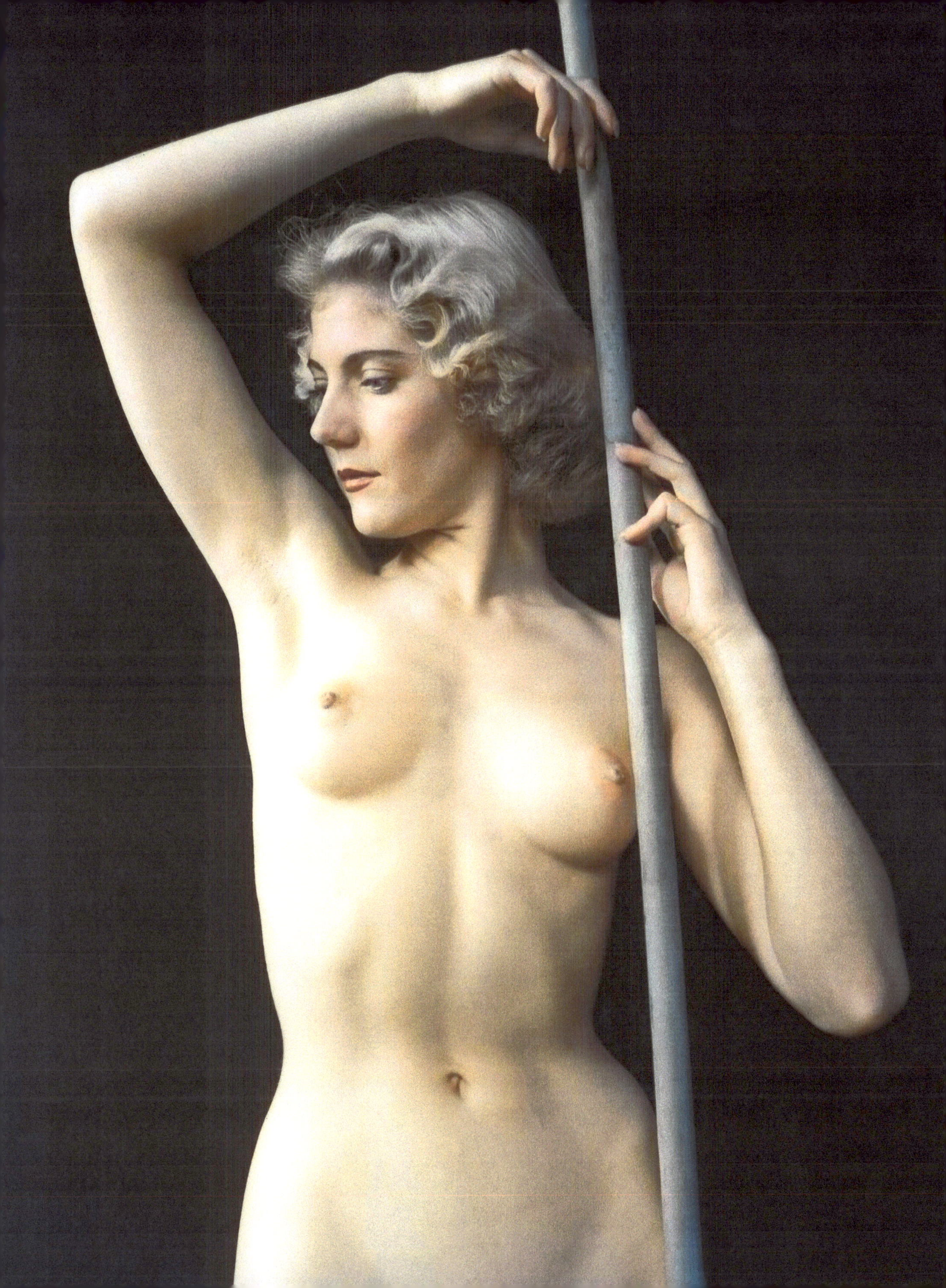

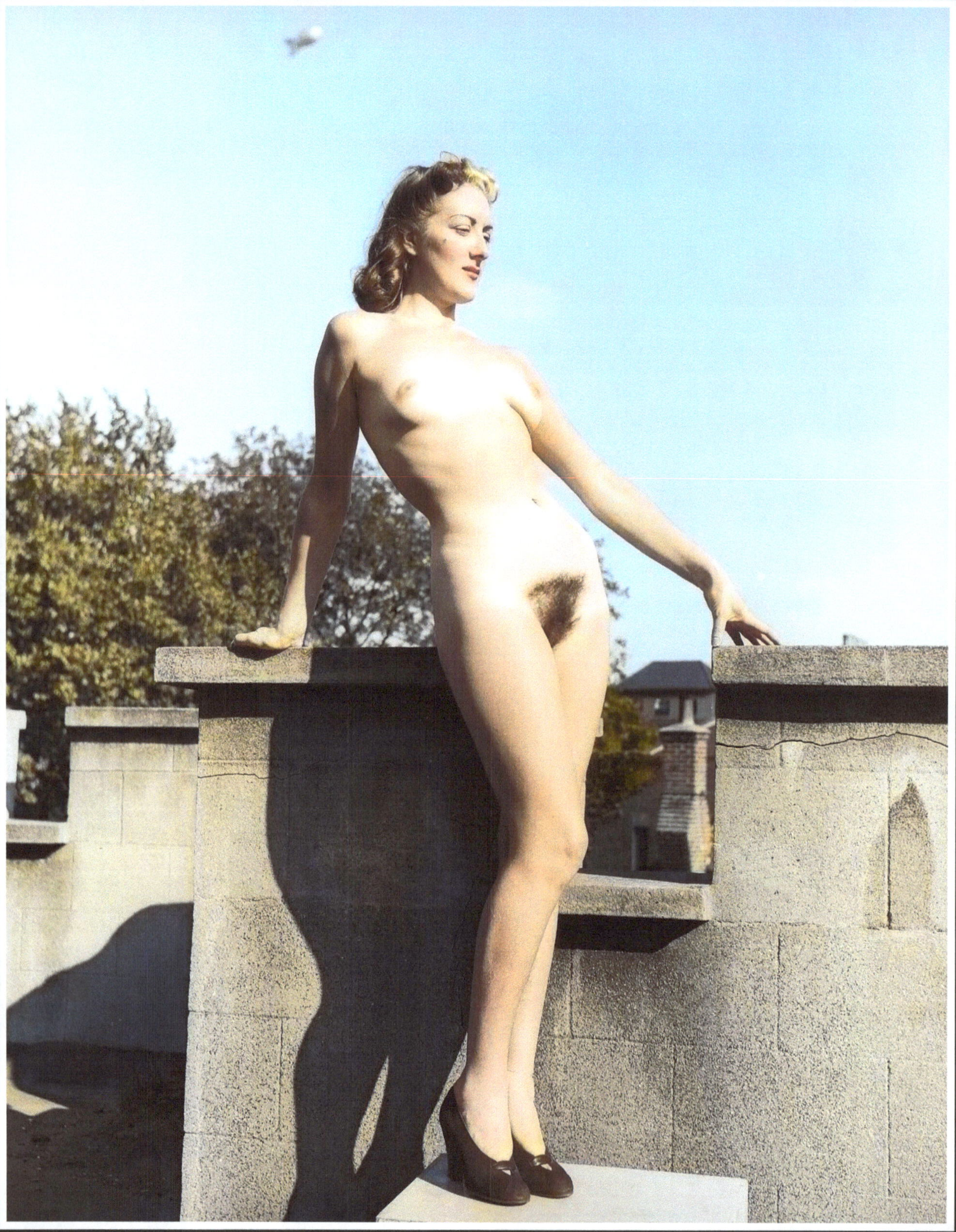

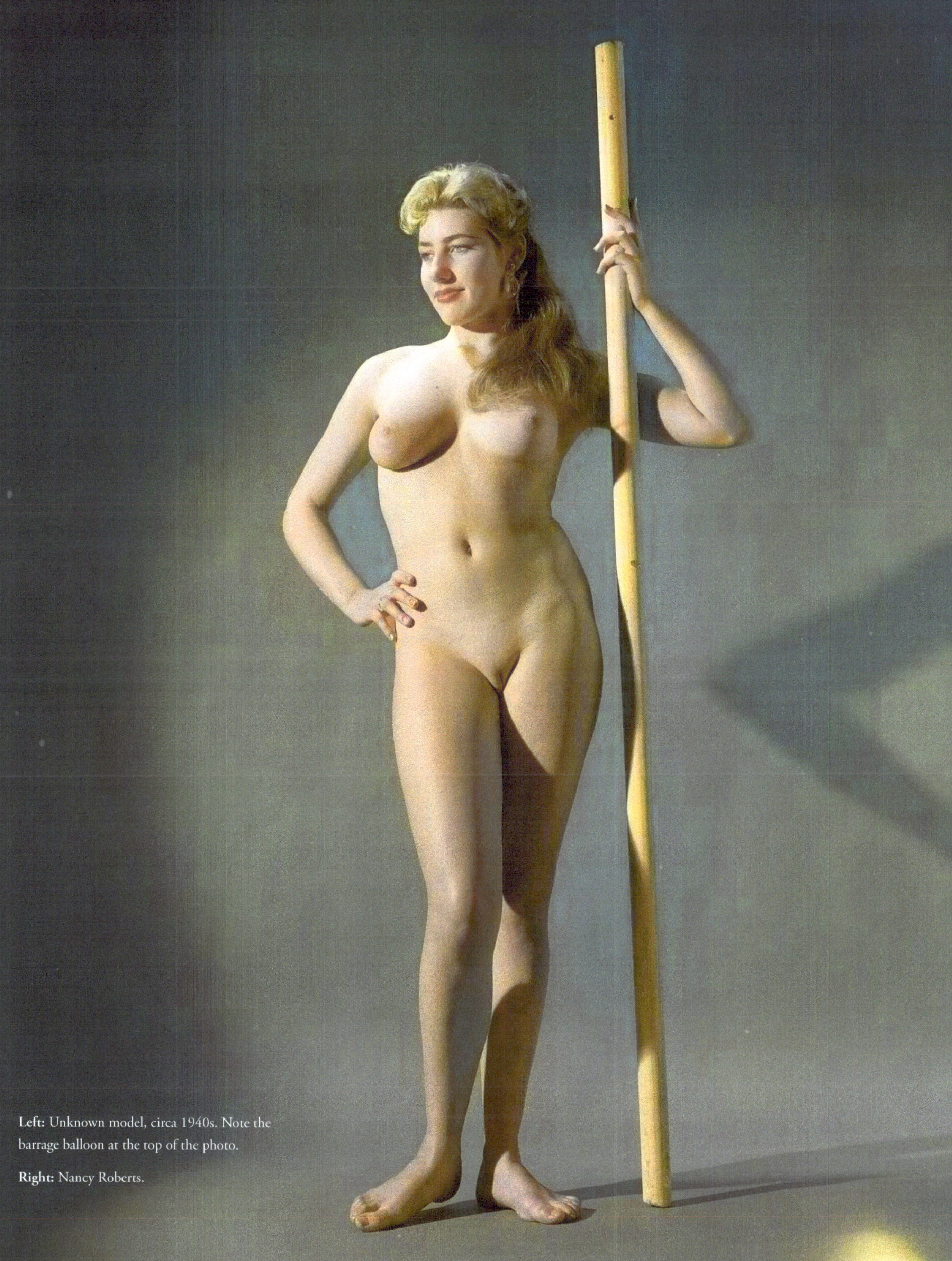

Left: Unknown model, circa 1940s. Note the
barrage balloon at the top of the photo.

Right: Nancy Roberts.

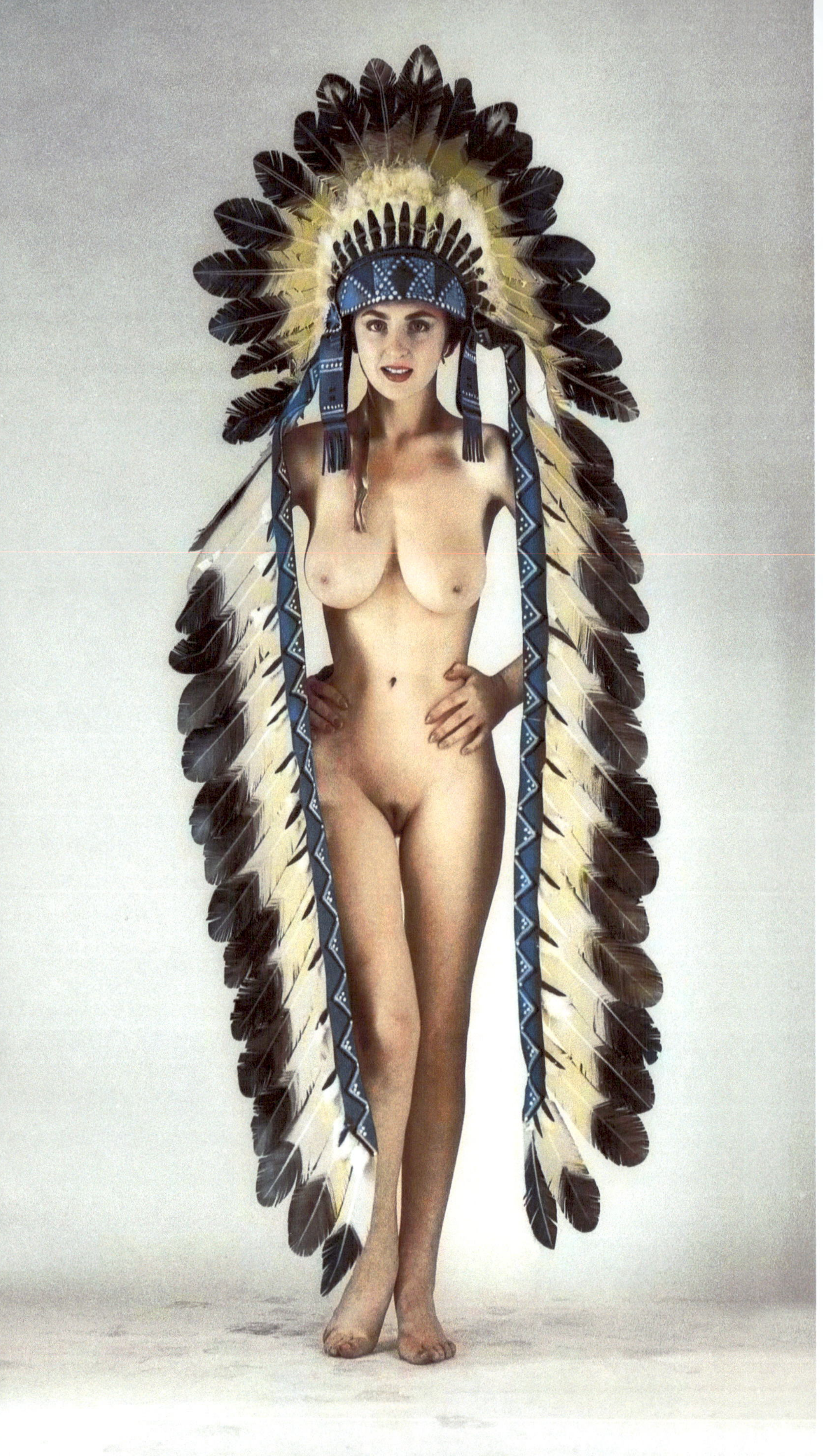

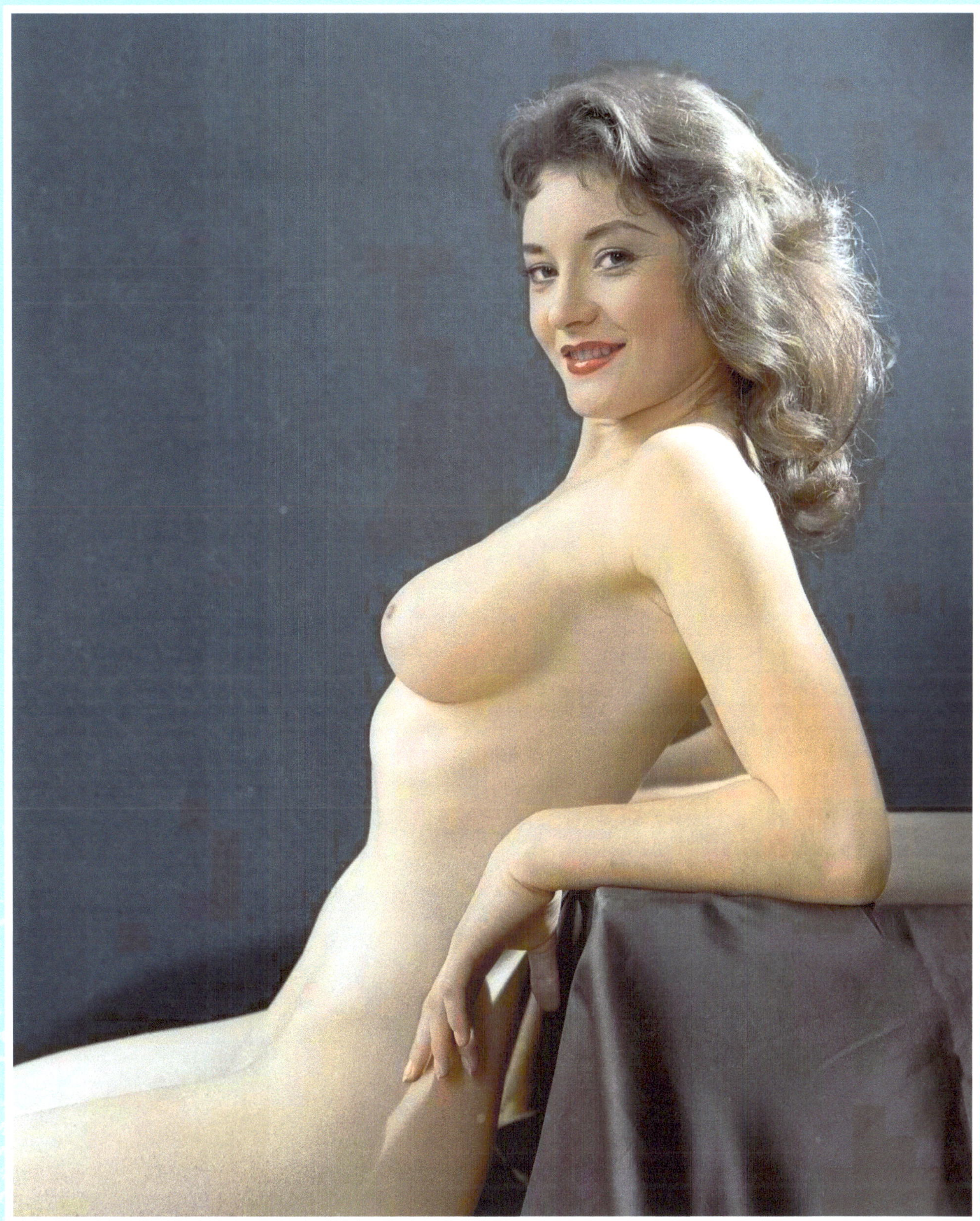

Above: Carole Richards **Left:** Ray Payne.

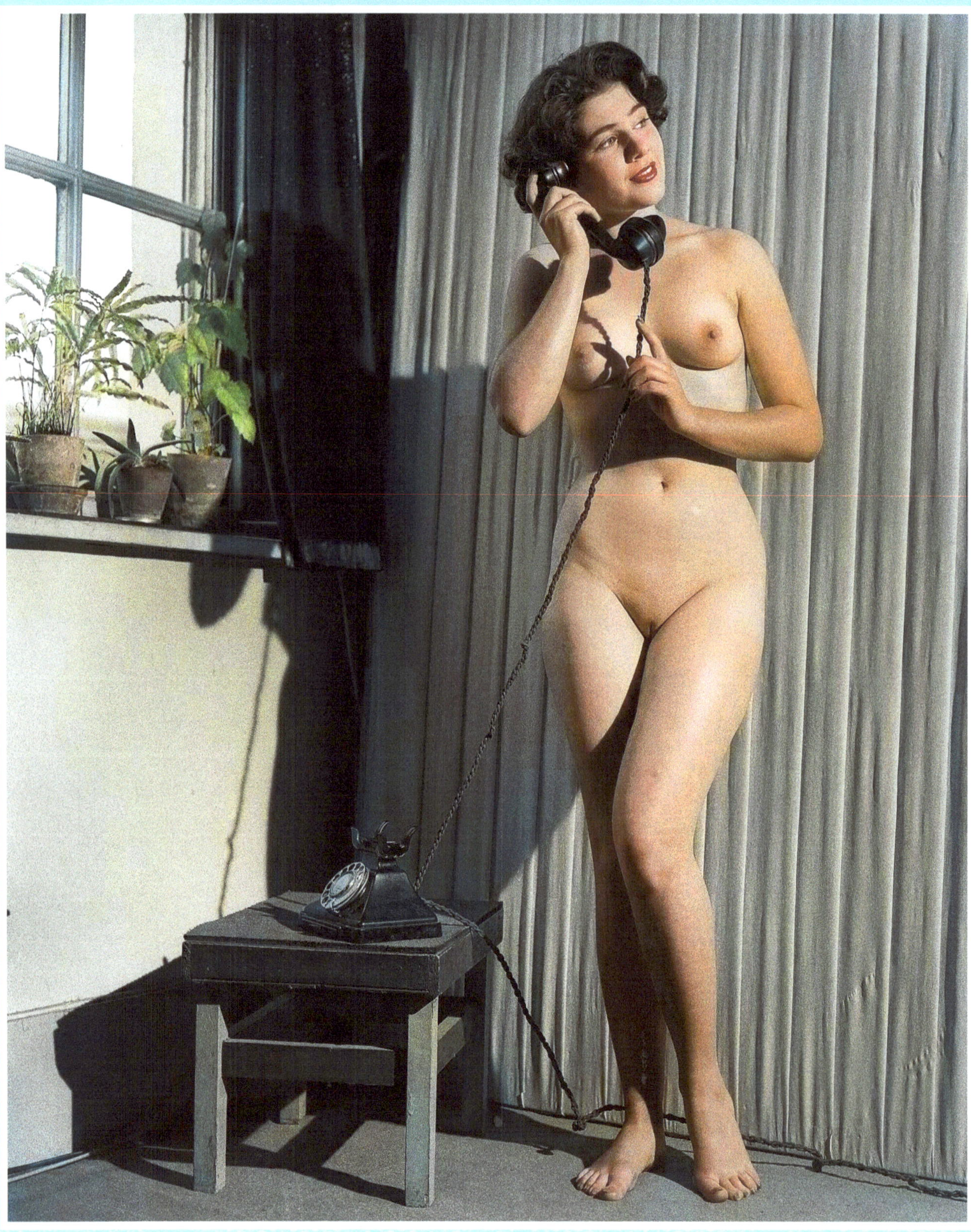

Above: Julie Alexander, a former receptionist from Fulham, London.

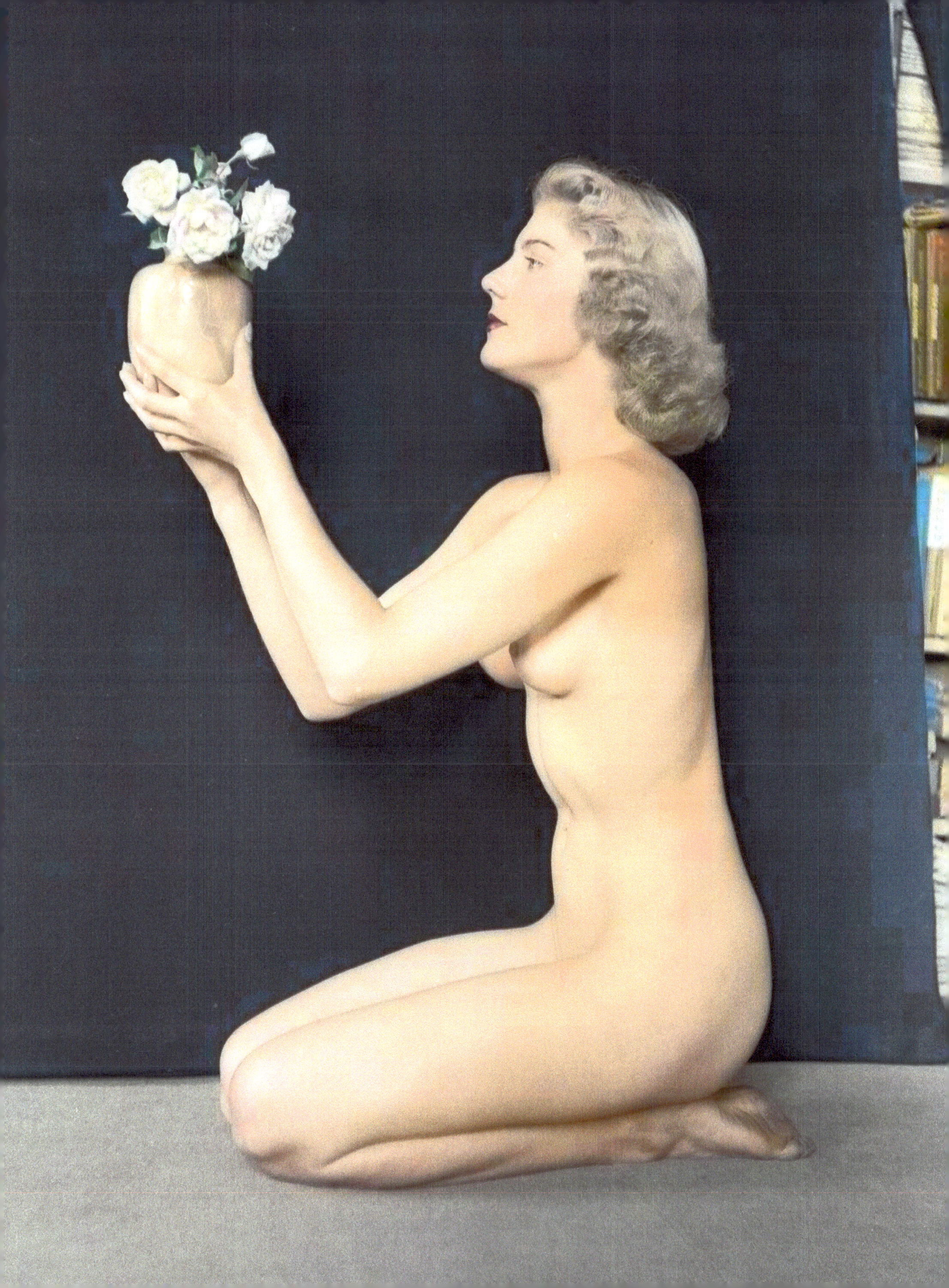

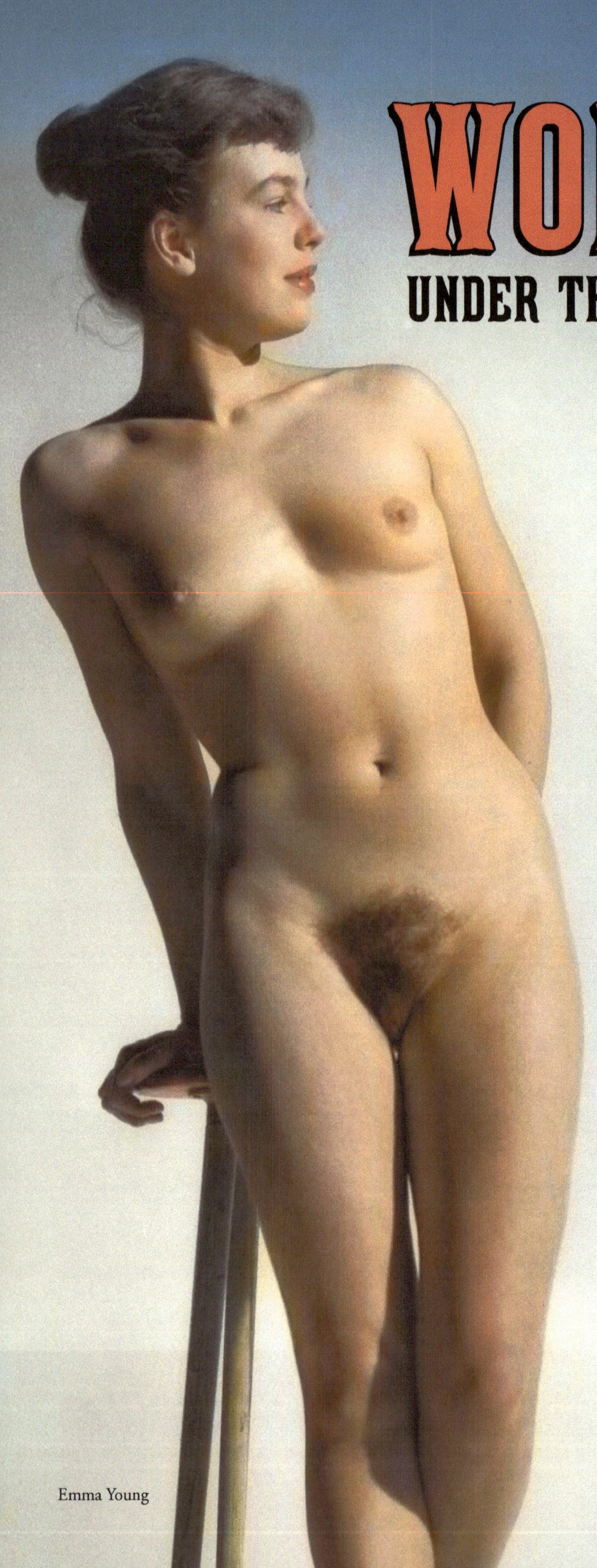

WOLFBAIT
UNDER THE COUNTER CULTURE

AVAILABLE TITLES

Cinema au Naturel
A history of nudist film.

Miniten: Rules of the Game
Invented in the 1930s, Miniten is a
tennis-like game played by naturists.

Naked as Nature Intended
The epic tale of a nudist picture by
Pamela Green, with photographs by
Douglas "Dambuster" Webb, DFM.

The Naked Truth About Harrison Marks
The notorious biography by Franklyn Wood.

Past Masters of the Nude
An illustrated bibliography of nude photography
books published in England from 1896 to 1960.

Slide Show
A luscious look at the photographic slides
of Harrison Marks.

X-ray Specs and Other Vintage Ads
A unique treasure chest of vintage advertising,
full of tease and prurient silliness.

Doing Rude Things
The history of the British sex film.

Emma Young

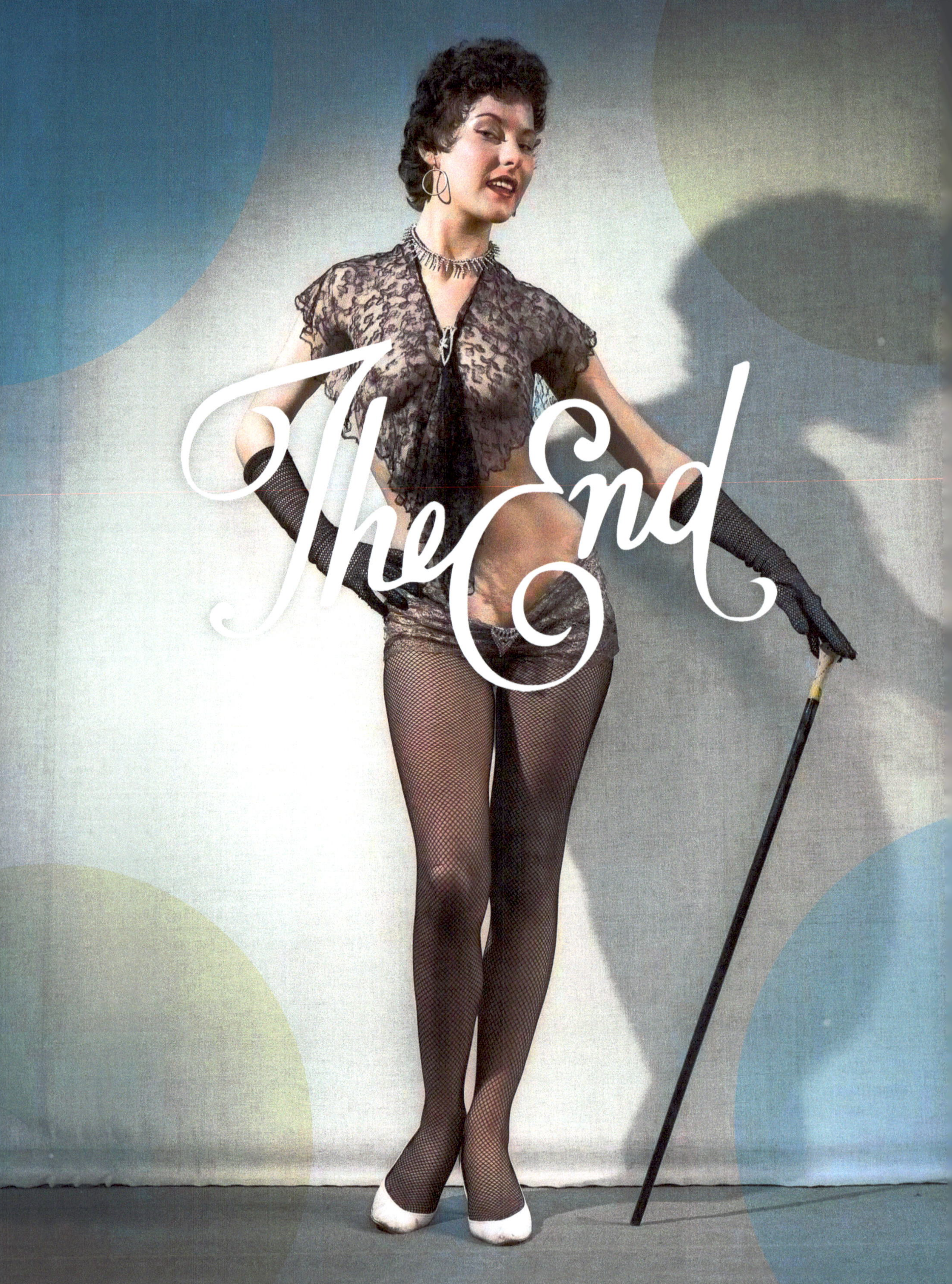
The End

9 781917 298063